The Syllabus of Errors Condemned by Pope Pius IX,
On the Doctrine of the Modernists
and The Syllabus of Modernist Errors
Condemned by Pope Saint Pius X

Pope Pius IX
Pope Saint Pius X

Table of Contents

THE SYLLABUS OF ERRORS CONDEMNED BY PIUS IX...................................5
PASCENDI DOMINICI GREGIS...19
SYLLABUS CONDEMNING THE ERRORS OF THE MODERNISTS................71

THE SYLLABUS OF ERRORS CONDEMNED BY PIUS IX

I. PANTHEISM, NATURALISM AND ABSOLUTE RATIONALISM

1. There exists no Supreme, all-wise, all-provident Divine Being, distinct from the universe, and God is identical with the nature of things, and is, therefore, subject to changes. In effect, God is produced in man and in the world, and all things are God and have the very substance of God, and God is one and the same thing with the world, and, therefore, spirit with matter, necessity with liberty, good with evil, justice with injustice. -- Allocution "Maxima quidem," June 9, 1862.

2. All action of God upon man and the world is to be denied. -- Ibid.

3. Human reason, without any reference whatsoever to God, is the sole arbiter of truth and falsehood, and of good and evil; it is law to itself, and suffices, by its natural force, to secure the welfare of men and of nations. -- Ibid.

4. All the truths of religion proceed from the innate strength of human reason; hence reason is the ultimate standard by which man can and ought to arrive at the knowledge of all truths of every kind. -- Ibid. and Encyclical "Qui pluribus," Nov. 9, 1846, etc.

5. Divine revelation is imperfect, and therefore subject to a continual and indefinite progress, corresponding with the advancement of human reason. -- Ibid.

6. The faith of Christ is in opposition to human reason and divine revelation not only is not useful, but is even hurtful to the perfection of man. -- Ibid.

7. The prophecies and miracles set forth and recorded in the Sacred Scriptures are the fiction of poets, and the mysteries of the Christian faith the result of philosophical investigations. In the books

of the Old and the New Testament there are contained mythical inventions, and Jesus Christ is Himself a myth.

II. MODERATE RATIONALISM

8. As human reason is placed on a level with religion itself, so theological must be treated in the same manner as philosophical sciences. -- Allocution "Singulari quadam," Dec. 9, 1854.

9. All the dogmas of the Christian religion are indiscriminately the object of natural science or philosophy, and human reason, enlightened solely in an historical way, is able, by its own natural strength and principles, to attain to the true science of even the most abstruse dogmas; provided only that such dogmas be proposed to reason itself as its object. -- Letters to the Archbishop of Munich, "Gravissimas inter," Dec. 11, 1862, and "Tuas libenter," Dec. 21, 1863.

10. As the philosopher is one thing, and philosophy another, so it is the right and duty of the philosopher to subject himself to the authority which he shall have proved to be true; but philosophy neither can nor ought to submit to any such authority. -- Ibid., Dec. 11, 1862.

11. The Church not only ought never to pass judgment on philosophy, but ought to tolerate the errors of philosophy, leaving it to correct itself. -- Ibid., Dec. 21, 1863.

12. The decrees of the Apostolic See and of the Roman congregations impede the true progress of science. -- Ibid.

13. The method and principles by which the old scholastic doctors cultivated theology are no longer suitable to the demands of our times and to the progress of the sciences. -- Ibid.

14. Philosophy is to be treated without taking any account of supernatural revelation. -- Ibid.

III. INDIFFERENTISM, LATITUDINARIANISM

15. Every man is free to embrace and profess that religion which, guided by the light of reason, he shall consider true. -- Allocution "Maxima quidem," June 9, 1862; Damnatio "Multiplices inter," June 10, 1851.

16. Man may, in the observance of any religion whatever, find the way of eternal salvation, and arrive at eternal salvation. -- Encyclical "Qui pluribus," Nov. 9, 1846.

17. Good hope at least is to be entertained of the eternal salvation of all those who are not at all in the true Church of Christ. -- Encyclical "Quanto conficiamur," Aug. 10, 1863, etc.

18. Protestantism is nothing more than another form of the same true Christian religion, in which form it is given to please God equally as in the Catholic Church. -- Encyclical "Noscitis," Dec. 8, 1849.

IV. SOCIALISM, COMMUNISM, SECRET SOCIETIES, BIBLICAL SOCIETIES, CLERICO-LIBERAL SOCIETIES

Pests of this kind are frequently reprobated in the severest terms in the Encyclical "Qui pluribus," Nov. 9, 1846, Allocution "Quibus quantisque," April 20, 1849, Encyclical "Noscitis et nobiscum," Dec. 8, 1849, Allocution "Singulari quadam," Dec. 9, 1854, Encyclical "Quanto conficiamur," Aug. 10, 1863.

V. ERRORS CONCERNING THE CHURCH AND HER RIGHTS

19. The Church is not a true and perfect society, entirely free- nor is she endowed with proper and perpetual rights of her own, conferred upon her by her Divine Founder; but it appertains to the civil power to define what are the rights of the Church, and the limits within which she may exercise those rights. -- Allocution "Singulari quadam," Dec. 9, 1854, etc.

20. The ecclesiastical power ought not to exercise its authority without the permission and assent of the civil government. -- Allocution "Meminit unusquisque," Sept. 30, 1861.

21. The Church has not the power of defining dogmatically that the religion of the Catholic Church is the only true religion. -- Damnatio "Multiplices inter," June 10, 1851.

22. The obligation by which Catholic teachers and authors are strictly bound is confined to those things only which are proposed to universal belief as dogmas of faith by the infallible judgment of the Church. -- Letter to the Archbishop of Munich, "Tuas libenter," Dec. 21, 1863.

23. Roman pontiffs and ecumenical councils have wandered outside the limits of their powers, have usurped the rights of princes, and have even erred in defining matters of faith and morals. -- Damnatio "Multiplices inter," June 10, 1851.

24. The Church has not the power of using force, nor has she any temporal power, direct or indirect. -- Apostolic Letter "Ad Apostolicae," Aug. 22, 1851.

25. Besides the power inherent in the episcopate, other temporal power has been attributed to it by the civil authority granted either explicitly or tacitly, which on that account is revocable by the civil authority whenever it thinks fit. -- Ibid.

26. The Church has no innate and legitimate right of acquiring and possessing property. -- Allocution "Nunquam fore," Dec. 15, 1856; Encyclical "Incredibili," Sept. 7, 1863.

27. The sacred ministers of the Church and the Roman pontiff are to be absolutely excluded from every charge and dominion over temporal affairs. -- Allocution "Maxima quidem," June 9, 1862.

28. It is not lawful for bishops to publish even letters Apostolic without the permission of Government. -- Allocution "Nunquam fore," Dec. 15, 1856.

29. Favours granted by the Roman pontiff ought to be considered null, unless they have been sought for through the civil government. -- Ibid.

30. The immunity of the Church and of ecclesiastical persons derived its origin from civil law. -- Damnatio "Multiplices inter," June 10, 1851.

31. The ecclesiastical forum or tribunal for the temporal causes, whether civil or criminal, of clerics, ought by all means to be abolished, even without consulting and against the protest of the Holy See. -- Allocution "Nunquam fore," Dec. 15, 1856; Allocution "Acerbissimum," Sept. 27, 1852.

32. The personal immunity by which clerics are exonerated from military conscription and service in the army may be abolished without violation either of natural right or equity. Its abolition is called for by civil progress, especially in a society framed on the model of a liberal government. -- Letter to the Bishop of Monreale "Singularis nobisque," Sept. 29, 1864.

33. It does not appertain exclusively to the power of ecclesiastical jurisdiction by right, proper and innate, to direct the teaching of theological questions. -- Letter to the Archbishop of Munich, "Tuas libenter," Dec. 21, 1863.

34. The teaching of those who compare the Sovereign Pontiff to a prince, free and acting in the universal Church, is a doctrine which prevailed in the Middle Ages. -- Apostolic Letter "Ad Apostolicae," Aug. 22, 1851.

35. There is nothing to prevent the decree of a general council, or the act of all peoples, from transferring the supreme pontificate

from the bishop and city of Rome to another bishop and another city. -- Ibid.

36. The definition of a national council does not admit of any subsequent discussion, and the civil authority car assume this principle as the basis of its acts. -- Ibid.

37. National churches, withdrawn from the authority of the Roman pontiff and altogether separated, can be established. -- Allocution "Multis gravibusque," Dec. 17, 1860.

38. The Roman pontiffs have, by their too arbitrary conduct, contributed to the division of the Church into Eastern and Western. -- Apostolic Letter "Ad Apostolicae," Aug. 22, 1851.

VI. ERRORS ABOUT CIVIL SOCIETY, CONSIDERED BOTH IN ITSELF AND IN ITS RELATION TO THE CHURCH

39. The State, as being the origin and source of all rights, is endowed with a certain right not circumscribed by any limits. -- Allocution "Maxima quidem," June 9, 1862.

40. The teaching of the Catholic Church is hostile to the well-being and interests of society. -- Encyclical "Qui pluribus," Nov. 9, 1846; Allocution "Quibus quantisque," April 20, 1849.

41. The civil government, even when in the hands of an infidel sovereign, has a right to an indirect negative power over religious affairs. It therefore possesses not only the right called that of "exsequatur," but also that of appeal, called "appellatio ab abusu." -- Apostolic Letter "Ad Apostolicae," Aug. 22, 1851

42. In the case of conflicting laws enacted by the two powers, the civil law prevails. -- Ibid.

43. The secular Dower has authority to rescind, declare and render null, solemn conventions, commonly called concordats, entered into with the Apostolic See, regarding the use of rights appertaining to

ecclesiastical immunity, without the consent of the Apostolic See, and even in spite of its protest. -- Allocution "Multis gravibusque," Dec. 17, 1860; Allocution "In consistoriali," Nov. 1, 1850.

44. The civil authority may interfere in matters relating to religion, morality and spiritual government: hence, it can pass judgment on the instructions issued for the guidance of consciences, conformably with their mission, by the pastors of the Church. Further, it has the right to make enactments regarding the administration of the divine sacraments, and the dispositions necessary for receiving them. -- Allocutions "In consistoriali," Nov. 1, 1850, and "Maxima quidem," June 9, 1862.

45. The entire government of public schools in which the youth-of a Christian state is educated, except (to a certain extent) in the case of episcopal seminaries, may and ought to appertain to the civil power, and belong to it so far that no other authority whatsoever shall be recognized as having any right to interfere in the discipline of the schools, the arrangement of the studies, the conferring of degrees, in the choice or approval of the teachers. -- Allocutions "Quibus luctuosissimis," Sept. 5, 1851, and "In consistoriali," Nov. 1, 1850.

46. Moreover, even in ecclesiastical seminaries, the method of studies to be adopted is subject to the civil authority. -- Allocution "Nunquam fore," Dec. 15, 1856.

47. The best theory of civil society requires that popular schools open to children of every class of the people, and, generally, all public institutes intended for instruction in letters and philosophical sciences and for carrying on the education of youth, should be freed from all ecclesiastical authority, control and interference, and should be fully subjected to the civil and political power at the pleasure of the rulers, and according to the standard of the prevalent opinions of the age. -- Epistle to the Archbishop of Freiburg, "Cum non sine," July 14, 1864.

48. Catholics may approve of the system of educating youth unconnected with Catholic faith and the power of the Church, and

which regards the knowledge of merely natural things, and only, or at least primarily, the ends of earthly social life. -- Ibid.

49. The civil power may prevent the prelates of the Church and the faithful from communicating freely and mutually with the Roman pontiff. -- Allocution "Maxima quidem," June 9, 1862.

50. Lay authority possesses of itself the right of presenting bishops, and may require of them to undertake the administration of the diocese before they receive canonical institution, and the Letters Apostolic from the Holy See. -- Allocution "Nunquam fore," Dec. 15, 1856.

51. And, further, the lay government has the right of deposing bishops from their pastoral functions, and is not bound to obey the Roman pontiff in those things which relate to the institution of bishoprics and the appointment of bishops. -- Allocution "Acerbissimum," Sept. 27, 1852, Damnatio "Multiplices inter," June 10, 1851.

52. Government can, by its own right, alter the age prescribed by the Church for the religious profession of women and men; and may require of all religious orders to admit no person to take solemn vows without its permission. -- Allocution "Nunquam fore," Dec. 15, 1856.

53. The laws enacted for the protection of religious orders and regarding their rights and duties ought to be abolished; nay, more, civil Government may lend its assistance to all who desire to renounce the obligation which they have undertaken of a religious life, and to break their vows. Government may also suppress the said religious orders, as likewise collegiate churches and simple benefices, even those of advowson and subject their property and revenues to the administration and pleasure of the civil power. -- Allocutions "Acerbissimum," Sept. 27, 1852; "Probe memineritis," Jan. 22, 1855; "Cum saepe," July 26, 1855.

54. Kings and princes are not only exempt from the jurisdiction of the Church, but are superior to the Church in deciding questions of jurisdiction. -- Damnatio "Multiplices inter," June 10, 1851.

55. The Church ought to be separated from the .State, and the State from the Church. -- Allocution "Acerbissimum," Sept. 27, 1852.

VII. ERRORS CONCERNING NATURAL AND CHRISTIAN ETHICS

56. Moral laws do not stand in need of the divine sanction, and it is not at all necessary that human laws should be made conformable to the laws of nature and receive their power of binding from God. -- Allocution "Maxima quidem," June 9, 1862.

57. The science of philosophical things and morals and also civil laws may and ought to keep aloof from divine and ecclesiastical authority. -- Ibid.

58. No other forces are to be recognized except those which reside in matter, and all the rectitude and excellence of morality ought to be placed in the accumulation and increase of riches by every possible means, and the gratification of pleasure. -- Ibid.; Encyclical "Quanto conficiamur," Aug. 10, 1863.

59. Right consists in the material fact. All human duties are an empty word, and all human facts have the force of right. -- Allocution "Maxima quidem," June 9, 1862.

60. Authority is nothing else but numbers and the sum total of material forces. -- Ibid.

61. The injustice of an act when successful inflicts no injury on the sanctity of right. -- Allocution "Jamdudum cernimus," March 18, 1861.

62. The principle of non-intervention, as it is called, ought to be proclaimed and observed. -- Allocution "Novos et ante," Sept. 28, 1860.

63. It is lawful to refuse obedience to legitimate princes, and even to rebel against them. -- Encyclical "Qui pluribus," Nov. 9, 1864; Allocution "Quibusque vestrum," Oct. 4, 1847; "Noscitis et Nobiscum," Dec. 8, 1849; Apostolic Letter "Cum Catholica."

64. The violation of any solemn oath, as well as any wicked and flagitious action repugnant to the eternal law, is not only not blamable but is altogether lawful and worthy of the highest praise when done through love of country. -- Allocution "Quibus quantisque," April 20, 1849.

VIII. ERRORS CONCERNING CHRISTIAN MARRIAGE

65. The doctrine that Christ has raised marriage to the dignity of a sacrament cannot be at all tolerated. -- Apostolic Letter "Ad Apostolicae," Aug. 22, 1851.

66. The Sacrament of Marriage is only a something accessory to the contract and separate from it, and the sacrament itself consists in the nuptial benediction alone. -- Ibid.

67. By the law of nature, the marriage tie is not indissoluble, and in many cases divorce properly so called may be decreed by the civil authority. -- Ibid.; Allocution "Acerbissimum," Sept. 27, 1852.

68. The Church has not the power of establishing diriment impediments of marriage, but such a power belongs to the civil authority by which existing impediments are to be removed. -- Damnatio "Multiplices inter," June 10, 1851.

69. In the dark ages the Church began to establish diriment impediments, not by her own right, but by using a power borrowed from the State. -- Apostolic Letter "Ad Apostolicae," Aug. 22, 1851.

70. The canons of the Council of Trent, which anathematize those who dare to deny to the Church the right of establishing diriment impediments, either are not dogmatic or must be understood as referring to such borrowed power. -- Ibid.

71. The form of solemnizing marriage prescribed by the Council of Trent, under pain of nullity, does not bind in cases where the civil law lays down another form, and declares that when this new form is used the marriage shall be valid.

72. Boniface VIII was the first who declared that the vow of chastity taken at ordination renders marriage void. -- Ibid.

73. In force of a merely civil contract there may exist between Christians a real marriage, and it is false to say either that the marriage contract between Christians is always a sacrament, or that there is no contract if the sacrament be excluded. -- Ibid.; Letter to the King of Sardinia, Sept. 9, 1852; Allocutions "Acerbissimum," Sept. 27, 1852, "Multis gravibusque," Dec. 17, 1860.

74. Matrimonial causes and espousals belong by their nature to civil tribunals. -- Encyclical "Qui pluribus," Nov. 9 1846; Damnatio "Multiplices inter," June 10, 1851, "Ad Apostolicae," Aug. 22, 1851; Allocution "Acerbissimum," Sept. 27, 1852.

IX. ERRORS REGARDING THE CIVIL POWER OF THE SOVEREIGN PONTIFF

75. The children of the Christian and Catholic Church are divided amongst themselves about the compatibility of the temporal with the spiritual power. -- "Ad Apostolicae," Aug. 22, 1851.

76. The abolition of the temporal power of which the Apostolic See is possessed would contribute in the greatest degree to the liberty and prosperity of the Church. -- Allocutions "Quibus quantisque," April 20, 1849, "Si semper antea," May 20, 1850.

X. ERRORS HAVING REFERENCE TO MODERN LIBERALISM

77. In the present day it is no longer expedient that the Catholic religion should be held as the only religion of the State, to the

exclusion of all other forms of worship. -- Allocution "Nemo vestrum," July 26, 1855.

78. Hence it has been wisely decided by law, in some Catholic countries, that persons coming to reside therein shall enjoy the public exercise of their own peculiar worship. -- Allocution "Acerbissimum," Sept. 27, 1852.

79. Moreover, it is false that the civil liberty of every form of worship, and the full power, given to all, of overtly and publicly manifesting any opinions whatsoever and thoughts, conduce more easily to corrupt the morals and minds of the people, and to propagate the pest of indifferentism. -- Allocution "Nunquam fore," Dec. 15, 1856.

80. The Roman Pontiff can, and ought to, reconcile himself, and come to terms with progress, liberalism and modern civilization.--Allocution "Jamdudum cernimus," March 18, 1861.

The faith teaches us and human reason demonstrates that a double order of things exists, and that we must therefore distinguish between the two earthly powers, the one of natural origin which provides for secular affairs and the tranquillity of human society, the other of supernatural origin, which presides over the City of God, that is to say the Church of Christ, which has been divinely instituted for the sake of souls and of eternal salvation.... The duties of this twofold power are most wisely ordered in such a way that to God is given what is God's (Matt. 22:21), and because of God to Caesar what is Caesar's, who is great because he is smaller than heaven. Certainly the Church has never disobeyed this divine command, the Church which always and everywhere instructs the faithful to show the respect which they should inviolably have for the supreme authority and its secular rights....

. . . Venerable Brethren, you see clearly enough how sad and full of perils is the condition of Catholics in the regions of Europe which We have mentioned. Nor are things any better or circumstances calmer in America, where some regions are so hostile to Catholics that their governments seem to deny by their actions the Catholic faith they claim to profess. In fact, there, for the last few years, a ferocious war on the Church, its institutions and the rights of the Apostolic See has been raging.... Venerable Brothers, it is surprising that in our time such a great war is being waged against the Catholic Church. But anyone who knows the nature, desires and intentions of the sects, whether they be called masonic or bear another name, and compares them with the nature the systems and the vastness of the obstacles by which the Church has been assailed almost everywhere, cannot doubt that the present misfortune must mainly be imputed to the frauds and machinations of these sects. It is from them that the synagogue of Satan, which gathers its troops against the Church of Christ, takes its strength. In the past Our predecessors, vigilant even from the beginning in Israel, had already denounced them to the kings and the nations, and had condemned them time and time again, and even We have not failed in this duty. If those who would have been able to avert such a deadly scourge had only had more faith in the supreme Pastors of the Church! But this scourge, winding through sinuous caverns, . . . deceiving many with astute frauds, finally has arrived at the point where it comes forth impetuously from its hiding places and triumphs as a powerful master. Since the throng of its propagandists has grown enormously, these wicked groups think that they have already become masters of the world and that they have almost reached their pre-established goal. Having sometimes obtained what they desired, and that is power, in several countries, they boldly turn the help of powers and authorities which they have secured to trying to submit the Church of God to the most cruel servitude, to undermine the foundations on which it rests, to contaminate its splendid qualities; and, moreover, to strike it with frequent blows, to shake it, to overthrow it, and, if possible, to make it disappear completely from the earth. Things being thus, Venerable Brothers, make every effort to defend the faithful which are entrusted to you against the insidious contagion of these sects and to save from perdition those who unfortunately have inscribed themselves in such sects. Make known and attack those who, whether suffering from, or planning, deception, are not afraid to affirm that these shady congregations aim only at the profit of society, at progress and mutual benefit. Explain to them often and impress deeply on their souls the Papal constitutions on this subject and teach, them that the masonic associations are anathematized by them not only in Europe but also in America and wherever they may be in the whole world.

To the Archbishops and Bishops of Prussia concerning the situation of the Catholic Church faced with persecution by that Government....

But although they (the bishops resisting persecution) should be praised rather than pitied, the scorn of episcopal dignity, the violation of the liberty and the rights of the Church, the ill treatment which does not only oppress those dioceses, but also the others of the Kingdom of Prussia, demand that We, owing to the Apostolic office with which God has entrusted us in spite of Our insufficient merit, protest against laws which have produced such great evils and make one fear even greater ones; and as far as we are able to do so with the sacred authority of divine law, We vindicate for the Church the freedom which has been trodden underfoot with sacrilegious violence. That is why by this letter we intend to do Our duty by announcing openly to all those whom this matter concerns and to the whole Catholic world, that these laws are null and void because they are absolutely contrary to the divine constitution of the Church. In fact, with respect to matters which concern the holy ministry, Our Lord did not put the mighty of this century in charge, but Saint Peter, whom he entrusted not only with feeding his sheep, but also the goats; therefore no power in the world, however great it may be, can deprive of the pastoral office those whom the Holy Ghost has made Bishops in order to feed the Church of God.

PASCENDI DOMINICI GREGIS

To the Patriarchs, Primates, Archbishops, Bishops and other Local Ordinaries in Peace and Communion with the Apostolic See.

Venerable Brethren, Health and Apostolic Benediction.

The office divinely committed to Us of feeding the Lord's flock has especially this duty assigned to it by Christ, namely, to guard with the greatest vigilance the deposit of the faith delivered to the saints, rejecting the profane novelties of words and oppositions of knowledge falsely so called. There has never been a time when this watchfulness of the supreme pastor was not necessary to the Catholic body; for, owing to the efforts of the enemy of the human race, there have never been lacking "men speaking perverse things" (Acts xx. 30), "vain talkers and seducers" (Tit. i. 10), "erring and driving into error" (2 Tim. iii. 13). Still it must be confessed that the number of the enemies of the cross of Christ has in these last days increased exceedingly, who are striving, by arts, entirely new and full of subtlety, to destroy the vital energy of the Church, and, if they can, to overthrow utterly Christ's kingdom itself. Wherefore We may no longer be silent, lest We should seem to fail in Our most sacred duty, and lest the kindness that, in the hope of wiser counsels, We have hitherto shown them, should be attributed to forgetfulness of Our office.

Gravity of the Situation

2. That We make no delay in this matter is rendered necessary especially by the fact that the partisans of error are to be sought not only among the Church's open enemies; they lie hid, a thing to be deeply deplored and feared, in her very bosom and heart, and are the more mischievous, the less conspicuously they appear. We allude, Venerable Brethren, to many who belong to the Catholic laity, nay, and this is far more lamentable, to the ranks of the priesthood itself, who, feigning a love for the Church, lacking the firm protection of philosophy and theology, nay more, thoroughly imbued with the poisonous doctrines taught by the enemies of the Church, and lost to all sense of modesty, vaunt themselves as reformers of the Church; and, forming more boldly into line of attack, assail all that is most sacred in the work of Christ, not sparing even the person of the Divine

Redeemer, whom, with sacrilegious daring, they reduce to a simple, mere man.

3. Though they express astonishment themselves, no one can justly be surprised that We number such men among the enemies of the Church, if, leaving out of consideration the internal disposition of soul, of which God alone is the judge, he is acquainted with their tenets, their manner of speech, their conduct. Nor indeed will he err in accounting them the most pernicious of all the adversaries of the Church. For as We have said, they put their designs for her ruin into operation not from without but from within; hence, the danger is present almost in the very veins and heart of the Church, whose injury is the more certain, the more intimate is their knowledge of her. Moreover they lay the axe not to the branches and shoots, but to the very root, that is, to the faith and its deepest fires. And having struck at this root of immortality, they proceed to disseminate poison through the whole tree, so that there is no part of Catholic truth from which they hold their hand, none that they do not strive to corrupt. Further, none is more skilful, none more astute than they, in the employment of a thousand noxious arts; for they double the parts of rationalist and Catholic, and this so craftily that they easily lead the unwary into error; and since audacity is their chief characteristic, there is no conclusion of any kind from which they shrink or which they do not thrust forward with pertinacity and assurance. To this must be added the fact, which indeed is well calculated to deceive souls, that they lead a life of the greatest activity, of assiduous and ardent application to every branch of learning, and that they possess, as a rule, a reputation for the strictest morality. Finally, and this almost destroys all hope of cure, their very doctrines have given such a bent to their minds, that they disdain all authority and brook no restraint; and relying upon a false conscience, they attempt to ascribe to a love of truth that which is in reality the result of pride and obstinacy.

Once indeed We had hopes of recalling them to a better sense, and to this end we first of all showed them kindness as Our children, then we treated them with severity, and at last We have had recourse, though with great reluctance, to public reproof. But you know, Venerable Brethren, how fruitless has been Our action. They bowed their head for a moment, but it was soon uplifted more arrogantly than ever. If it were a matter which concerned them alone, We might perhaps have overlooked it: but the security of the Catholic name is at stake. Wherefore, as to maintain it longer would be a crime, We must now break silence, in order to expose before the whole Church in their true colours those men who have assumed this bad disguise.

Division of the Encyclical

4. But since the Modernists (as they are commonly and rightly called) employ a very clever artifice, namely, to present their doctrines without order and systematic arrangement into one whole, scattered and disjointed one from another, so as to appear to be in doubt and uncertainty, while they are in reality firm and steadfast, it will be of advantage, Venerable Brethren, to bring their teachings together here into one group, and to point out the connexion between them, and thus to pass to an examination of the sources of the errors, and to prescribe remedies for averting the evil.

ANALYSIS OF MODERNIST TEACHING

5. To proceed in an orderly manner in this recondite subject, it must first of all be noted that every Modernist sustains and comprises within himself many personalities; he is a philosopher, a believer, a theologian, an historian, a critic, an apologist, a reformer. These roles must be clearly distinguished from one another by all who would accurately know their system and thoroughly comprehend the principles and the consequences of their doctrines.

Agnosticism its Philosophical Foundation

6. We begin, then, with the philosopher. Modernists place the foundation of religious philosophy in that doctrine which is usually called Agnosticism. According to this teaching human reason is confined entirely within the field of phenomena, that is to say, to things that are perceptible to the senses, and in the manner in which they are perceptible; it has no right and no power to transgress these limits. Hence it is incapable of lifting itself up to God, and of recognising His existence, even by means of visible things. From this it is inferred that God can never be the direct object of science, and that,

as regards history, He must not be considered as an historical subject. Given these premises, all will readily perceive what becomes of Natural Theology, of the motives of credibility, of external revelation. The Modernists simply make away with them altogether; they include them in Intellectualism, which they call a ridiculous and long ago defunct system. Nor does the fact that the Church has formally condemned these portentous errors exercise the slightest restraint upon them. Yet the Vatican Council has defined, "If anyone says that the one true God, our Creator and Lord, cannot be known with certainty by the natural light of human reason by means of the things that are made, let him be anathema" (De Revel., can. I); and also: "If anyone says that it is not possible or not expedient that man be taught, through the medium of divine revelation, about God and the worship to be paid Him, let him be anathema" (Ibid., can. 2); and finally, "If anyone says that divine revelation cannot be made credible by external signs, and that therefore men should be drawn to the faith only by their personal internal experience or by private inspiration, let him be anathema" (De Fide, can. 3). But how the Modernists make the transition from Agnosticism, which is a state of pure nescience, to scientific and historic Atheism, which is a doctrine of positive denial; and consequently, by what legitimate process of reasoning, starting from ignorance as to whether God has in fact intervened in the history of the human race or not, they proceed, in their explanation of this history, to ignore God altogether, as if He really had not intervened, let him answer who can. Yet it is a fixed and established principle among them that both science and history must be atheistic: and within their boundaries there is room for nothing but phenomena; God and all that is divine are utterly excluded. We shall soon see clearly what, according to this most absurd teaching, must be held touching the most sacred Person of Christ, what concerning the mysteries of His life and death, and of His Resurrection and Ascension into heaven.

Vital Immanence

7. However, this Agnosticism is only the negative part of the system of the Modernist: the positive side of it consists in what they call vital immanence. This is how they advance from one to the other. Religion, whether natural or supernatural, must, like every other fact,

admit of some explanation. But when Natural theology has been destroyed, the road to revelation closed through the rejection of the arguments of credibility, and all external revelation absolutely denied, it is clear that this explanation will be sought in vain outside man himself. It must, therefore, be looked for in man; and since religion is a form of life, the explanation must certainly be found in the life of man. Hence the principle of religious immanence is formulated. Moreover, the first actuation, so to say, of every vital phenomenon, and religion, as has been said, belongs to this category, is due to a certain necessity or impulsion; but it has its origin, speaking more particularly of life, in a movement of the heart, which movement is called a sentiment. Therefore, since God is the object of religion, we must conclude that faith, which is the basis and the foundation of all religion, consists in a sentiment which originates from a need of the divine. This need of the divine, which is experienced only in special and favourable circumstances, cannot, of itself, appertain to the domain of consciousness; it is at first latent within the consciousness, or, to borrow a term from modern philosophy, in the subconsciousness, where also its roots lies hidden and undetected.

Should anyone ask how it is that this need of the divine which man experiences within himself grows up into a religion, the Modernists reply thus: Science and history, they say, are confined within two limits, the one external, namely, the visible world, the other internal, which is consciousness. When one or other of these boundaries has been reached, there can be no further progress, for beyond is the unknowable. In presence of this unknowable, whether it is outside man and beyond the visible world of nature, or lies hidden within in the subconsciousness, the need of the divine, according to the principles of Fideism, excites in a soul with a propensity towards religion a certain special sentiment, without any previous advertence of the mind: and this sentiment possesses, implied within itself both as its own object and as its intrinsic cause, the reality of the divine, and in a way unites man with God. It is this sentiment to which Modernists give the name of faith, and this it is which they consider the beginning of religion.

8. But we have not yet come to the end of their philosophy, or, to speak more accurately, their folly. For Modernism finds in this sentiment not faith only, but with and in faith, as they understand it,

revelation, they say, abides. For what more can one require for revelation? Is not that religious sentiment which is perceptible in the consciousness revelation, or at least the beginning of revelation? Nay, is not God Himself, as He manifests Himself to the soul, indistinctly it is true, in this same religious sense, revelation? And they add: Since God is both the object and the cause of faith, this revelation is at the same time of God and from God; that is, God is both the revealer and the revealed.

Hence, Venerable Brethren, springs that ridiculous proposition of the Modernists, that every religion, according to the different aspect under which it is viewed, must be considered as both natural and supernatural. Hence it is that they make consciousness and revelation synonymous. Hence the law, according to which religious consciousness is given as the universal rule, to be put on an equal footing with revelation, and to which all must submit, even the supreme authority of the Church, whether in its teaching capacity, or in that of legislator in the province of sacred liturgy or discipline.

Deformation of Religious History the Consequence

9. However, in all this process, from which, according to the Modernists, faith and revelation spring, one point is to be particularly noted, for it is of capital importance on account of the historico-critical corollaries which are deduced from it. - For the Unknowable they talk of does not present itself to faith as something solitary and isolated; but rather in close conjunction with some phenomenon, which, though it belongs to the realm of science and history yet to some extent oversteps their bounds. Such a phenomenon may be an act of nature containing within itself something mysterious; or it may be a man, whose character, actions and words cannot, apparently, be reconciled with the ordinary laws of history. Then faith, attracted by the Unknowable which is united with the phenomenon, possesses itself of the whole phenomenon, and, as it were, permeates it with its own life. From this two things follow. The first is a sort of transfiguration of the phenomenon, by its elevation above its own true conditions, by which it becomes more adapted to that form of the divine which faith will infuse into it. The second is a kind of disfigurement, which springs from the fact that faith, which has made the phenomenon independent

of the circumstances of place and time, attributes to it qualities which it has not; and this is true particularly of the phenomena of the past, and the older they are, the truer it is. From these two principles the Modernists deduce two laws, which, when united with a third which they have already got from agnosticism, constitute the foundation of historical criticism. We will take an illustration from the Person of Christ. In the person of Christ, they say, science and history encounter nothing that is not human. Therefore, in virtue of the first canon deduced from agnosticism, whatever there is in His history suggestive of the divine, must be rejected. Then, according to the second canon, the historical Person of Christ was transfigured by faith; therefore everything that raises it above historical conditions must be removed. Lately, the third canon, which lays down that the person of Christ has been disfigured by faith, requires that everything should be excluded, deeds and words and all else that is not in keeping with His character, circumstances and education, and with the place and time in which He lived. A strange style of reasoning, truly; but it is Modernist criticism.

10. Therefore the religious sentiment, which through the agency of vital immanence emerges from the lurking places of the subconsciousness, is the germ of all religion, and the explanation of everything that has been or ever will be in any religion. The sentiment, which was at first only rudimentary and almost formless, gradually matured, under the influence of that mysterious principle from which it originated, with the progress of human life, of which, as has been said, it is a form. This, then, is the origin of all religion, even supernatural religion; it is only a development of this religious sentiment. Nor is the Catholic religion an exception; it is quite on a level with the rest; for it was engendered, by the process of vital immanence, in the consciousness of Christ, who was a man of the choicest nature, whose like has never been, nor will be. - Those who hear these audacious, these sacrilegious assertions, are simply shocked! And yet, Venerable Brethren, these are not merely the foolish babblings of infidels. There are many Catholics, yea, and priests too, who say these things openly; and they boast that they are going to reform the Church by these ravings! There is no question now of the old error, by which a sort of right to the supernatural order was claimed for the human nature. We have gone far beyond that: we have reached the point when it is affirmed that our most holy religion, in the

man Christ as in us, emanated from nature spontaneously and entirely. Than this there is surely nothing more destructive of the whole supernatural order. Wherefore the Vatican Council most justly decreed: "If anyone says that man cannot be raised by God to a knowledge and perfection which surpasses nature, but that he can and should, by his own efforts and by a constant development, attain finally to the possession of all truth and good, let him be anathema" (De Revel., can. 3).

The Origin of Dogmas

11. So far, Venerable Brethren, there has been no mention of the intellect. Still it also, according to the teaching of the Modernists, has its part in the act of faith. And it is of importance to see how. - In that sentiment of which We have frequently spoken, since sentiment is not knowledge, God indeed presents Himself to man, but in a manner so confused and indistinct that He can hardly be perceived by the believer. It is therefore necessary that a ray of light should be cast upon this sentiment, so that God may be clearly distinguished and set apart from it. This is the task of the intellect, whose office it is to reflect and to analyse, and by means of which man first transforms into mental pictures the vital phenomena which arise within him, and then expresses them in words. Hence the common saying of Modernists: that the religious man must ponder his faith. - The intellect, then, encountering this sentiment directs itself upon it, and produces in it a work resembling that of a painter who restores and gives new life to a picture that has perished with age. The simile is that of one of the leaders of Modernism. The operation of the intellect in this work is a double one: first by a natural and spontaneous act it expresses its concept in a simple, ordinary statement; then, on reflection and deeper consideration, or, as they say, by elaborating its thought, it expresses the idea in secondary propositions, which are derived from the first, but are more perfect and distinct. These secondary propositions, if they finally receive the approval of the supreme magisterium of the Church, constitute dogma.

12. Thus, We have reached one of the principal points in the Modernists' system, namely the origin and the nature of dogma. For they place the origin of dogma in those primitive and simple formulae,

which, under a certain aspect, are necessary to faith; for revelation, to be truly such, requires the clear manifestation of God in the consciousness. But dogma itself they apparently hold, is contained in the secondary formulae.

To ascertain the nature of dogma, we must first find the relation which exists between the religious formulas and the religious sentiment. This will be readily perceived by him who realises that these formulas have no other purpose than to furnish the believer with a means of giving an account of his faith to himself. These formulas therefore stand midway between the believer and his faith; in their relation to the faith, they are the inadequate expression of its object, and are usually called symbols; in their relation to the believer, they are mere instruments.

Its Evolution

13. Hence it is quite impossible to maintain that they express absolute truth: for, in so far as they are symbols, they are the images of truth, and so must be adapted to the religious sentiment in its relation to man; and as instruments, they are the vehicles of truth, and must therefore in their turn be adapted to man in his relation to the religious sentiment. But the object of the religious sentiment, since it embraces that absolute, possesses an infinite variety of aspects of which now one, now another, may present itself. In like manner, he who believes may pass through different phases. Consequently, the formulae too, which we call dogmas, must be subject to these vicissitudes, and are, therefore, liable to change. Thus the way is open to the intrinsic evolution of dogma. An immense collection of sophisms this, that ruins and destroys all religion. Dogma is not only able, but ought to evolve and to be changed. This is strongly affirmed by the Modernists, and as clearly flows from their principles. For amongst the chief points of their teaching is this which they deduce from the principle of vital immanence; that religious formulas, to be really religious and not merely theological speculations, ought to be living and to live the life of the religious sentiment. This is not to be understood in the sense that these formulas, especially if merely imaginative, were to be made for the religious sentiment; it has no more to do with their origin than with number or quality; what is

necessary is that the religious sentiment, with some modification when necessary, should vitally assimilate them. In other words, it is necessary that the primitive formula be accepted and sanctioned by the heart; and similarly the subsequent work from which spring the secondary formulas must proceed under the guidance of the heart. Hence it comes that these formulas, to be living, should be, and should remain, adapted to the faith and to him who believes. Wherefore if for any reason this adaptation should cease to exist, they lose their first meaning and accordingly must be changed. And since the character and lot of dogmatic formulas is so precarious, there is no room for surprise that Modernists regard them so lightly and in such open disrespect. And so they audaciously charge the Church both with taking the wrong road from inability to distinguish the religious and moral sense of formulas from their surface meaning, and with clinging tenaciously and vainly to meaningless formulas whilst religion is allowed to go to ruin. Blind that they are, and leaders of the blind, inflated with a boastful science, they have reached that pitch of folly where they pervert the eternal concept of truth and the true nature of the religious sentiment; with that new system of theirs they are seen to be under the sway of a blind and unchecked passion for novelty, thinking not at all of finding some solid foundation of truth, but despising the holy and apostolic traditions, they embrace other vain, futile, uncertain doctrines, condemned by the Church, on which, in the height of their vanity, they think they can rest and maintain truth itself.

The Modernist as Believer:
Individual Experience and Religious Certitude

14. Thus far, Venerable Brethren, of the Modernist considered as Philosopher. Now if we proceed to consider him as Believer, seeking to know how the Believer, according to Modernism, is differentiated from the Philosopher, it must be observed that although the Philosopher recognises as the object of faith the divine reality, still this reality is not to be found but in the heart of the Believer, as being an object of sentiment and affirmation; and therefore confined within the sphere of phenomena; but as to whether it exists outside that sentiment and affirmation is a matter which in no way concerns this

Philosopher. For the Modernist .Believer, on the contrary, it is an established and certain fact that the divine reality does really exist in itself and quite independently of the person who believes in it. If you ask on what foundation this assertion of the Believer rests, they answer: In the experience of the individual. On this head the Modernists differ from the Rationalists only to fall into the opinion of the Protestants and pseudo-mystics. This is their manner of putting the question: In the religious sentiment one must recognise a kind of intuition of the heart which puts man in immediate contact with the very reality of God, and infuses such a persuasion of God's existence and His action both within and without man as to excel greatly any scientific conviction. They assert, therefore, the existence of a real experience, and one of a kind that surpasses all rational experience. If this experience is denied by some, like the rationalists, it arises from the fact that such persons are unwilling to put themselves in the moral state which is necessary to produce it. It is this experience which, when a person acquires it, makes him properly and truly a believer.

How far off we are here from Catholic teaching we have already seen in the decree of the Vatican Council. We shall see later how, with such theories, added to the other errors already mentioned, the way is opened wide for atheism. Here it is well to note at once that, given this doctrine of experience united with the other doctrine of symbolism, every religion, even that of paganism, must be held to be true. What is to prevent such experiences from being met within every religion? In fact that they are to be found is asserted by not a few. And with what right will Modernists deny the truth of an experience affirmed by a follower of Islam? With what right can they claim true experiences for Catholics alone? Indeed Modernists do not deny but actually admit, some confusedly, others in the most open manner, that all religions are true. That they cannot feel otherwise is clear. For on what ground, according to their theories, could falsity be predicated of any religion whatsoever? It must be certainly on one of these two: either on account of the falsity of the religious sentiment or on account of the falsity of the formula pronounced by the mind. Now the religious sentiment, although it may be more perfect or less perfect, is always one and the same; and the intellectual formula, in order to be true, has but to respond to the religious sentiment and to the Believer, whatever be the intellectual capacity of the latter. In the conflict between different

29

religions, the most that Modernists can maintain is that the Catholic has more truth because it is more living and that it deserves with more reason the name of Christian because it corresponds more fully with the origins of Christianity. That these consequences flow from the premises will not seem unnatural to anybody. But what is amazing is that there are Catholics and priests who, We would fain believe, abhor such enormities yet act as if they fully approved of them. For they heap such praise and bestow such public honour on the teachers of these errors as to give rise to the belief that their admiration is not meant merely for the persons, who are perhaps not devoid of a certain merit, but rather for the errors which these persons openly profess and which they do all in their power to propagate.

Religious Experience and Tradition

15. But this doctrine of experience is also under another aspect entirely contrary to Catholic truth. It is extended and applied to tradition, as hitherto understood by the Church, and destroys it. By the Modernists, tradition is understood as a communication to others, through preaching by means of the intellectual formula, of an original experience. To this formula, in addition to its representative value, they attribute a species of suggestive efficacy which acts both in the person who believes, to stimulate the religious sentiment should it happen to have grown sluggish and to renew the experience once acquired, and in those who do not yet believe, to awake for the first time the religious sentiment in them and to produce the experience. In this way is religious experience propagated among the peoples; and not merely among contemporaries by preaching, but among future generations both by books and by oral transmission from one to another. Sometimes this communication of religious experience takes root and thrives, at other times it withers at once and dies. For the Modernists, to live is a proof of truth, since for them life and truth are one and the same thing. Hence again it is given to us to infer that all existing religions are equally true, for otherwise they would not live.

Faith and Science

16. Having reached this point, Venerable Brethren, we have sufficient material in hand to enable us to see the relations which Modernists establish between faith and science, including history also under the name of science. And in the first place it is to be held that the object of the one is quite extraneous to and separate from the object of the other. For faith occupies itself solely with something which science declares to be unknowable for it. Hence each has a separate field assigned to it: science is entirely concerned with the reality of phenomena, into which faith does not enter at all; faith on the contrary concerns itself with the divine reality which is entirely unknown to science. Thus the conclusion is reached that there can never be any dissension between faith and science, for if each keeps on its own ground they can never meet and therefore never be in contradiction. And if it be objected that in the visible world there are some things which appertain to faith, such as the human life of Christ, the Modernists reply by denying this. For though such things come within the category of phenomena, still in as far as they are lived by faith and in the way already described have been by faith transfigured and disfigured, they have been removed from the world of sense and translated to become material for the divine. Hence should it be further asked whether Christ has wrought real miracles, and made real prophecies, whether He rose truly from the dead and ascended into heaven, the answer of agnostic science will be in the negative and the answer of faith in the affirmative - yet there will not be, on that account, any conflict between them. For it will be denied by the philosopher as philosopher, speaking to philosophers and considering Christ only in His historical reality; and it will be affirmed by the speaker, speaking to believers and considering the life of Christ as lived again by the faith and in the faith.

Faith Subject to Science

17. Yet, it would be a great mistake to suppose that, given these theories, one is authorised to believe that faith and science are independent of one another. On the side of science the independence is indeed complete, but it is quite different with regard to faith, which is subject to science not on one but on three grounds. For in the first place it must be observed that in every religious fact, when you take

away the divine reality and the experience of it which the believer possesses, everything else, and especially the religious formulas of it, belongs to the sphere of phenomena and therefore falls under the control of science. Let the believer leave the world if he will, but so long as he remains in it he must continue, whether he like it or not, to be subject to the laws, the observation, the judgments of science and of history. Further, when it is said that God is the object of faith alone, the statement refers only to the divine reality not to the idea of God. The latter also is subject to science which while it philosophises in what is called the logical order soars also to the absolute and the ideal. It is therefore the right of philosophy and of science to form conclusions concerning the idea of God, to direct it in its evolution and to purify it of any extraneous elements which may become confused with it. Finally, man does not suffer a dualism to exist in him, and the believer therefore feels within him an impelling need so to harmonise faith with science, that it may never oppose the general conception which science sets forth concerning the universe.

Thus it is evident that science is to be entirely independent of faith, while on the other hand, and notwithstanding that they are supposed to be strangers to each other, faith is made subject to science. All this, Venerable Brothers, is in formal opposition with the teachings of Our Predecessor, Pius IX, where he lays it down that: In matters of religion it is the duty of philosophy not to command but to serve, but not to prescribe what is to be believed but to embrace what is to be believed with reasonable obedience, not to scrutinise the depths of the mysteries of God but to venerate them devoutly and humbly.

The Modernists completely invert the parts, and to them may be applied the words of another Predecessor of Ours, Gregory IX., addressed to some theologians of his time: Some among you, inflated like bladders with the spirit of vanity strive by profane novelties to cross the boundaries fixed by the Fathers, twisting the sense of the heavenly pages . . .to the philosophical teaching of the rationals, not for the profit of their hearer but to make a show of science . . . these, seduced by strange and eccentric doctrines, make the head of the tail and force the queen to serve the servant.

The Methods of Modernists

18. This becomes still clearer to anybody who studies the conduct of Modernists, which is in perfect harmony with their teachings. In the writings and addresses they seem not unfrequently to advocate now one doctrine now another so that one would be disposed to regard them as vague and doubtful. But there is a reason for this, and it is to be found in their ideas as to the mutual separation of science and faith. Hence in their books you find some things which might well be expressed by a Catholic, but in the next page you find other things which might have been dictated by a rationalist. When they write history they make no mention of the divinity of Christ, but when they are in the pulpit they profess it clearly; again, when they write history they pay no heed to the Fathers and the Councils, but when they catechise the people, they cite them respectfully. In the same way they draw their distinctions between theological and pastoral exegesis and scientific and historical exegesis. So, too, acting on the principle that science in no way depends upon faith, when they treat of philosophy, history, criticism, feeling no horror at treading in the footsteps of Luther, they are wont to display a certain contempt for Catholic doctrines, or the Holy Fathers, for the Ecumenical Councils, for the ecclesiastical magisterium; and should they be rebuked for this, they complain that they are being deprived of their liberty. Lastly, guided by the theory that faith must be subject to science, they continuously and openly criticise the Church because of her sheer obstinacy in refusing to submit and accommodate her dogmas to the opinions of philosophy; while they, on their side, after having blotted out the old theology, endeavour to introduce a new theology which shall follow the vagaries of their philosophers.

The Modernist as Theologian:
His Principles, Immanence and Symbolism

19. And thus, Venerable Brethren, the road is open for us to study the Modernists in the theological arena - a difficult task, yet one that may be disposed of briefly. The end to be attained is the conciliation of faith with science, always, however, saving the primacy of science over faith. In this branch the Modernist theologian avails himself of exactly the same principles which we have seen employed by the Modernist philosopher, and applies them to the believer: the

principles of immanence and symbolism. The process is an extremely simple one. The philosopher has declared: The principle of faith is immanent; the believer has added: This principle is God; and the theologian draws the conclusion: God is immanent in man. Thus we have theological immanence. So too, the philosopher regards as certain that the representations of the object of faith are merely symbolical; the believer has affirmed that the object of faith is God in Himself; and the theologian proceeds to affirm that: The representations of the divine reality are symbolical. And thus we have theological symbolism. Truly enormous errors both, the pernicious character of which will be seen clearly from an examination of their consequences. For, to begin with symbolism, since symbols are but symbols in regard to their objects and only instruments in regard to the believer, it is necessary first of all, according to the teachings of the Modernists, that the believer do not lay too much stress on the formula, but avail himself of it only with the scope of uniting himself to the absolute truth which the formula at once reveals and conceals, that is to say, endeavours to express but without succeeding in doing so. They would also have the believer avail himself of the formulas only in as far as they are useful to him, for they are given to be a help and not a hindrance; with proper regard, however, for the social respect due to formulas which the public magisterium has deemed suitable for expressing the common consciousness until such time as the same magisterium provide otherwise. Concerning immanence it is not easy to determine what Modernists mean by it, for their own opinions on the subject vary. Some understand it in the sense that God working in man is more intimately present in him than man is in even himself, and this conception, if properly understood, is free from reproach. Others hold that the divine action is one with the action of nature, as the action of the first cause is one with the action of the secondary cause, and this would destroy the supernatural order. Others, finally, explain it in a way which savours of pantheism and this, in truth, is the sense which tallies best with the rest of their doctrines.

20. With this principle of immanence is connected another which may be called the principle of divine permanence. It differs from the first in much the same way as the private experience differs from the experience transmitted by tradition. An example will illustrate what is meant, and this example is offered by the Church and the

Sacraments. The Church and the Sacraments, they say, are not to be regarded as having been instituted by Christ Himself. This is forbidden by agnosticism, which sees in Christ nothing more than a man whose religious consciousness has been, like that of all men, formed by degrees; it is also forbidden by the law of immanence which rejects what they call external application; it is further forbidden by the law of evolution which requires for the development of the germs a certain time and a certain series of circumstances; it is, finally, forbidden by history, which shows that such in fact has been the course of things. Still it is to be held that both Church and Sacraments have been founded mediately by Christ. But how? In this way: All Christian consciences were, they affirm, in a manner virtually included in the conscience of Christ as the plant is included in the seed. But as the shoots live the life of the seed, so, too, all Christians are to be said to live the life of Christ. But the life of Christ is according to faith, and so, too, is the life of Christians. And since this life produced, in the courses of ages, both the Church and the Sacraments, it is quite right to say that their origin is from Christ and is divine. In the same way they prove that the Scriptures and the dogmas are divine. And thus the Modernistic theology may be said to be complete. No great thing, in truth, but more than enough for the theologian who professes that the conclusions of science must always, and in all things, be respected. The application of these theories to the other points We shall proceed to expound, anybody may easily make for himself.

Dogma and the Sacraments

21. Thus far We have spoken of the origin and nature of faith. But as faith has many shoots, and chief among them the Church, dogma, worship, the Books which we call "Sacred," of these also we must know what is taught by the Modernists. To begin with dogma, we have already indicated its origin and nature. Dogma is born of the species of impulse or necessity by virtue of which the believer is constrained to elaborate his religious thought so as to render it clearer for himself and others. This elaboration consists entirely in the process of penetrating and refining the primitive formula, not indeed in itself and according to logical development, but as required by circumstances, or vitally as the Modernists more abstrusely put it.

Hence it happens that around the primitive formula secondary formulas gradually continue to be formed, and these subsequently grouped into bodies of doctrine, or into doctrinal constructions as they prefer to call them, and further sanctioned by the public magisterium as responding to the common consciousness, are called dogma. Dogma is to be carefully distinguished from the speculations of theologians which, although not alive with the life of dogma, are not without their utility as serving to harmonise religion with science and remove opposition between the two, in such a way as to throw light from without on religion, and it may be even to prepare the matter for future dogma. Concerning worship there would not be much to be said, were it not that under this head are comprised the Sacraments, concerning which the Modernists fall into the gravest errors. For them the Sacraments are the resultant of a double need - for, as we have seen, everything in their system is explained by inner impulses or necessities. In the present case, the first need is that of giving some sensible manifestation to religion; the second is that of propagating it, which could not be done without some sensible form and consecrating acts, and these are called sacraments. But for the Modernists the Sacraments are mere symbols or signs, though not devoid of a certain efficacy - an efficacy, they tell us, like that of certain phrases vulgarly described as having "caught on," inasmuch as they have become the vehicle for the diffusion of certain great ideas which strike the public mind. What the phrases are to the ideas, that the Sacraments are to the religious sentiment - that and nothing more. The Modernists would be speaking more clearly were they to affirm that the Sacraments are instituted solely to foster the faith - but this is condemned by the Council of Trent: If anyone say that these sacraments are instituted solely to foster the faith, let him be anathema.

The Holy Scriptures

22. We have already touched upon the nature and origin of the Sacred Books. According to the principles of the Modernists they may be rightly described as a collection of experiences, not indeed of the kind that may come to anybody, but those extraordinary and striking ones which have happened in any religion. And this is precisely what they teach about our books of the Old and New Testament. But to suit

their own theories they note with remarkable ingenuity that, although experience is something belonging to the present, still it may derive its material from the past and the future alike, inasmuch as the believer by memory lives the past over again after the manner of the present, and lives the future already by anticipation. This explains how it is that the historical and apocalyptical books are included among the Sacred Writings. God does indeed speak in these books - through the medium of the believer, but only, according to Modernistic theology, by vital immanence and permanence. Do we inquire concerning inspiration? Inspiration, they reply, is distinguished only by its vehemence from that impulse which stimulates the believer to reveal the faith that is in him by words or writing. It is something like what happens in poetical inspiration, of which it has been said: There is God in us, and when he stirreth he sets us afire. And it is precisely in this sense that God is said to be the origin of the inspiration of the Sacred Books. The Modernists affirm, too, that there is nothing in these books which is not inspired. In this respect some might be disposed to consider them as more orthodox than certain other moderns who somewhat restrict inspiration, as, for instance, in what have been put forward as tacit citations. But it is all mere juggling of words. For if we take the Bible, according to the tenets of agnosticism, to be a human work, made by men for men, but allowing the theologian to proclaim that it is divine by immanence, what room is there left in it for inspiration? General inspiration in the Modernist sense it is easy to find, but of inspiration in the Catholic sense there is not a trace.

The Church

23. A wider field for comment is opened when you come to treat of the vagaries devised by the Modernist school concerning the Church. You must start with the supposition that the Church has its birth in a double need, the need of the individual believer, especially if he has had some original and special experience, to communicate his faith to others, and the need of the mass, when the faith has become common to many, to form itself into a society and to guard, increase, and propagate the common good. What, then, is the Church? It is the product of the collective conscience, that is to say of the society of individual consciences which by virtue of the principle of vital

permanence, all depend on one first believer, who for Catholics is Christ. Now every society needs a directing authority to guide its members towards the common end, to conserve prudently the elements of cohesion which in a religious society are doctrine and worship.

Hence the triple authority in the Catholic Church, disciplinary, dogmatic, liturgical. The nature of this authority is to be gathered from its origin, and its rights and duties from its nature. In past times it was a common error that authority came to the Church from without, that is to say directly from God; and it was then rightly held to be autocratic. But his conception had now grown obsolete. For in the same way as the Church is a vital emanation of the collectivity of consciences, so too authority emanates vitally from the Church itself. Authority therefore, like the Church, has its origin in the religious conscience, and, that being so, is subject to it. Should it disown this dependence it becomes a tyranny. For we are living in an age when the sense of liberty has reached its fullest development, and when the public conscience has in the civil order introduced popular government. Now there are not two consciences in man, any more than there are two lives. It is for the ecclesiastical authority, therefore, to shape itself to democratic forms, unless it wishes to provoke and foment an intestine conflict in the consciences of mankind. The penalty of refusal is disaster. For it is madness to think that the sentiment of liberty, as it is now spread abroad, can surrender. Were it forcibly confined and held in bonds, terrible would be its outburst, sweeping away at once both Church and religion. Such is the situation for the Modernists, and their one great anxiety is, in consequence, to find a way of conciliation between the authority of the Church and the liberty of believers.

The Relations Between Church and State

24. But it is not with its own members alone that the Church must come to an amicable arrangement - besides its relations with those within, it has others outside. The Church does not occupy the world all by itself; there are other societies in the world, with which it must necessarily have contact and relations. The rights and duties of the Church towards civil societies must, therefore, be determined, and

determined, of course, by its own nature as it has been already described. The rules to be applied in this matter are those which have been laid down for science and faith, though in the latter case the question is one of objects while here we have one of ends. In the same way, then, as faith and science are strangers to each other by reason of the diversity of their objects, Church and State are strangers by reason of the diversity of their ends, that of the Church being spiritual while that of the State is temporal. Formerly it was possible to subordinate the temporal to the spiritual and to speak of some questions as mixed, allowing to the Church the position of queen and mistress in all such, because the Church was then regarded as having been instituted immediately by God as the author of the supernatural order. But his doctrine is today repudiated alike by philosophy and history. The State must, therefore, be separated from the Church, and the Catholic from the citizen. Every Catholic, from the fact that he is also a citizen, has the right and the duty to work for the common good in the way he thinks best, without troubling himself about the authority of the Church, without paying any heed to its wishes, its counsels, its orders - nay, even in spite of its reprimands. To trace out and prescribe for the citizen any line of conduct, on any pretext whatsoever, is to be guilty of an abuse of ecclesiastical authority, against which one is bound to act with all one's might. The principles from which these doctrines spring have been solemnly condemned by our predecessor Pius VI. in his Constitution Auctorem fidei.

The Magisterium of the Church

25. But it is not enough for the Modernist school that the State should be separated from the Church. For as faith is to be subordinated to science, as far as phenomenal elements are concerned, so too in temporal matters the Church must be subject to the State. They do not say this openly as yet - but they will say it when they wish to be logical on this head. For given the principle that in temporal matters the State possesses absolute mastery, it will follow that when the believer, not fully satisfied with his merely internal acts of religion, proceeds to external acts, such for instance as the administration or reception of the sacraments, these will fall under the control of the State. What will then become of ecclesiastical authority, which can only be exercised by

external acts? Obviously it will be completely under the dominion of the State. It is this inevitable consequence which impels many among liberal Protestants to reject all external worship, nay, all external religious community, and makes them advocate what they call, individual religion. If the Modernists have not yet reached this point, they do ask the Church in the meanwhile to be good enough to follow spontaneously where they lead her and adapt herself to the civil forms in vogue. Such are their ideas about disciplinary authority. But far more advanced and far more pernicious are their teachings on doctrinal and dogmatic authority. This is their conception of the magisterium of the Church: No religious society, they say, can be a real unit unless the religious conscience of its members be one, and one also the formula which they adopt. But his double unity requires a kind of common mind whose office is to find and determine the formula that corresponds best with the common conscience, and it must have moreover an authority sufficient to enable it to impose on the community the formula which has been decided upon. From the combination and, as it were fusion of these two elements, the common mind which draws up the formula and the authority which imposes it, arises, according to the Modernists, the notion of the ecclesiastical magisterium. And as this magisterium springs, in its last analysis, from the individual consciences and possesses its mandate of public utility for their benefit, it follows that the ecclesiastical magisterium must be subordinate to them, and should therefore take democratic forms. To prevent individual consciences from revealing freely and openly the impulses they feel, to hinder criticism from impelling dogmas towards their necessary evolutions - this is not a legitimate use but an abuse of a power given for the public utility. So too a due method and measure must be observed in the exercise of authority. To condemn and prescribe a work without the knowledge of the author, without hearing his explanations, without discussion, assuredly savours of tyranny. And thus, here again a way must be found to save the full rights of authority on the one hand and of liberty on the other. In the meanwhile the proper course for the Catholic will be to proclaim publicly his profound respect for authority - and continue to follow his own bent. Their general directions for the Church may be put in this way: Since the end of the Church is entirely spiritual, the religious authority should strip itself of all that external pomp which adorns it in the eyes of the public.

And here they forget that while religion is essentially for the soul, it is not exclusively for the soul, and that the honour paid to authority is reflected back on Jesus Christ who instituted it.

The Evolution of Doctrine

26. To finish with this whole question of faith and its shoots, it remains to be seen, Venerable Brethren, what the Modernists have to say about their development. First of all they lay down the general principle that in a living religion everything is subject to change, and must change, and in this way they pass to what may be said to be, among the chief of their doctrines, that of Evolution. To the laws of evolution everything is subject - dogma, Church, worship, the Books we revere as sacred, even faith itself, and the penalty of disobedience is death. The enunciation of this principle will not astonish anybody who bears in mind what the Modernists have had to say about each of these subjects. Having laid down this law of evolution, the Modernists themselves teach us how it works out. And first with regard to faith. The primitive form of faith, they tell us, was rudimentary and common to all men alike, for it had its origin in human nature and human life. Vital evolution brought with it progress, not by the accretion of new and purely adventitious forms from without, but by an increasing penetration of the religious sentiment in the conscience. This progress was of two kinds: negative, by the elimination of all foreign elements, such, for example, as the sentiment of family or nationality; and positive by the intellectual and moral refining of man, by means of which the idea was enlarged and enlightened while the religious sentiment became more elevated and more intense. For the progress of faith no other causes are to be assigned than those which are adduced to explain its origin. But to them must be added those religious geniuses whom we call prophets, and of whom Christ was the greatest; both because in their lives and their words there was something mysterious which faith attributed to the divinity, and because it fell to their lot to have new and original experiences fully in harmony with the needs of their time. The progress of dogma is due chiefly to the obstacles which faith has to surmount, to the enemies it has to vanquish, to the contradictions it has to repel. Add to this a perpetual striving to penetrate ever more profoundly its own mysteries. Thus, to

omit other examples, has it happened in the case of Christ: in Him that divine something which faith admitted in Him expanded in such a way that He was at last held to be God. The chief stimulus of evolution in the domain of worship consists in the need of adapting itself to the uses and customs of peoples, as well as the need of availing itself of the value which certain acts have acquired by long usage. Finally, evolution in the Church itself is fed by the need of accommodating itself to historical conditions and of harmonising itself with existing forms of society. Such is religious evolution in detail. And here, before proceeding further, we would have you note well this whole theory of necessities and needs, for it is at the root of the entire system of the Modernists, and it is upon it that they will erect that famous method of theirs called the historical.

27. Still continuing the consideration of the evolution of doctrine, it is to be noted that Evolution is due no doubt to those stimulants styled needs, but, if left to their action alone, it would run a great risk of bursting the bounds of tradition, and thus, turned aside from its primitive vital principle, would lead to ruin instead of progress. Hence, studying more closely the ideas of the Modernists, evolution is described as resulting from the conflict of two forces, one of them tending towards progress, the other towards conservation. The conserving force in the Church is tradition, and tradition is represented by religious authority, and this both by right and in fact; for by right it is in the very nature of authority to protect tradition, and, in fact, for authority, raised as it is above the contingencies of life, feels hardly, or not at all, the spurs of progress. The progressive force, on the contrary, which responds to the inner needs lies in the individual consciences and ferments there - especially in such of them as are in most intimate contact with life. Note here, Venerable Brethren, the appearance already of that most pernicious doctrine which would make of the laity a factor of progress in the Church. Now it is by a species of compromise between the forces of conservation and of progress, that is to say between authority and individual consciences, that changes and advances take place. The individual consciences of some of them act on the collective conscience, which brings pressure to bear on the depositaries of authority, until the latter consent to a compromise, and, the pact being made, authority sees to its maintenance.

With all this in mind, one understands how it is that the Modernists express astonishment when they are reprimanded or punished. What is imputed to them as a fault they regard as a sacred duty. Being in intimate contact with consciences they know better than anybody else, and certainly better than the ecclesiastical authority, what needs exist - nay, they embody them, so to speak, in themselves. Having a voice and a pen they use both publicly, for this is their duty. Let authority rebuke them as much as it pleases - they have their own conscience on their side and an intimate experience which tells them with certainty that what they deserve is not blame but praise. Then they reflect that, after all there is no progress without a battle and no battle without its victim, and victims they are willing to be like the prophets and Christ Himself. They have no bitterness in their hearts against the authority which uses them roughly, for after all it is only doing its duty as authority. Their sole grief is that it remains deaf to their warnings, because delay multiplies the obstacles which impede the progress of souls, but the hour will most surely come when there will be no further chance for tergiversation, for if the laws of evolution may be checked for a while, they cannot be ultimately destroyed. And so they go their way, reprimands and condemnations notwithstanding, masking an incredible audacity under a mock semblance of humility. While they make a show of bowing their heads, their hands and minds are more intent than ever on carrying out their purposes. And this policy they follow willingly and wittingly, both because it is part of their system that authority is to be stimulated but not dethroned, and because it is necessary for them to remain within the ranks of the Church in order that they may gradually transform the collective conscience - thus unconsciously avowing that the common conscience is not with them, and that they have no right to claim to be its interpreters.

28. Thus then, Venerable Brethren, for the Modernists, both as authors and propagandists, there is to be nothing stable, nothing immutable in the Church. Nor indeed are they without precursors in their doctrines, for it was of these that Our Predecessor Pius IX wrote: These enemies of divine revelation extol human progress to the skies, and with rash and sacrilegious daring would have it introduced into the Catholic religion as if this religion were not the work of God but of man, or some kind of philosophical discovery susceptible of perfection

by human efforts. On the subject of revelation and dogma in particular, the doctrine of the Modernists offers nothing new - we find it condemned in the Syllabus of Pius IX., where it is enunciated in these terms: Divine revelation is imperfect, and therefore subject to continual and indefinite progress, corresponding with the progress of human reason; and condemned still more solemnly in the Vatican Council: The doctrine of the faith which God has revealed has not been proposed to human intelligences to be perfected by them as if it were a philosophical system, but as a divine deposit entrusted to the Spouse of Christ to be faithfully guarded and infallibly interpreted. Hence the sense, too, of the sacred dogmas is that which our Holy Mother the Church has once declared, nor is this sense ever to be abandoned on plea or pretext of a more profound comprehension of the truth. Nor is the development of our knowledge, even concerning the faith, impeded by this pronouncement - on the contrary it is aided and promoted. For the same Council continues: Let intelligence and science and wisdom, therefore, increase and progress abundantly and vigorously in individuals and in the mass, in the believer and in the whole Church, throughout the ages and the centuries - but only in its own kind, that is, according to the same dogma, the same sense, the same acceptation.

The Modernist as Historian and Critic

29. After having studied the Modernist as philosopher, believer and theologian, it now remains for us to consider him as historian, critic, apologist, reformer.

30. Some Modernists, devoted to historical studies, seem to be greatly afraid of being taken for philosophers. About philosophy, they tell you, they know nothing whatever - and in this they display remarkable astuteness, for they are particularly anxious not to be suspected of being prejudiced in favour of philosophical theories which would lay them open to the charge of not being objective, to use the word in vogue. And yet the truth is that their history and their criticism are saturated with their philosophy, and that their historico-critical conclusions are the natural fruit of their philosophical principles. This will be patent to anybody who reflects. Their three first laws are contained in those three principles of their philosophy already

dealt with: the principle of agnosticism, the principle of the transfiguration of things by faith, and the principle which We have called of disfiguration. Let us see what consequences flow from each of them. Agnosticism tells us that history, like ever other science, deals entirely with phenomena, and the consequence is that God, and every intervention of God in human affairs, is to be relegated to the domain of faith as belonging to it alone. In things where a double element, the divine and the human, mingles, in Christ, for example, or the Church, or the sacraments, or the many other objects of the same kind, a division must be made and the human element assigned to history while the divine will go to faith. Hence we have that distinction, so current among the Modernists, between the Christ of history and the Christ of faith, between the sacraments of history and the sacraments of faith, and so on. Next we find that the human element itself, which the historian has to work on, as it appears in the documents, has been by faith transfigured, that is to say raised above its historical conditions. It becomes necessary, therefore, to eliminate also the accretions which faith has added, to assign them to faith itself and to the history of faith: thus, when treating of Christ, the historian must set aside all that surpasses man in his natural condition, either according to the psychological conception of him, or according to the place and period of his existence. Finally, by virtue of the third principle, even those things which are not outside the sphere of history they pass through the crucible, excluding from history and relegating to faith everything which, in their judgment, is not in harmony with what they call the logic of facts and in character with the persons of whom they are predicated. Thus, they will not allow that Christ ever uttered those things which do not seem to be within the capacity of the multitudes that listened to Him. Hence they delete from His real history and transfer to faith all the allegories found in His discourses. Do you inquire as to the criterion they adopt to enable them to make these divisions? The reply is that they argue from the character of the man, from his condition of life, from his education, from the circumstances under which the facts took place - in short, from criteria which, when one considers them well, are purely subjective. Their method is to put themselves into the position and person of Christ, and then to attribute to Him what they would have done under like circumstances. In this way, absolutely a priori and acting on philosophical principles which they admit they hold but which they affect to ignore, they proclaim that Christ, according to what they call His real history, was not God and never did anything divine, and that as man He did and said only what they, judging from the time in which he lived, can admit Him to have said or done.

Criticism and its Principles

31. And as history receives its conclusions, ready-made, from philosophy, so too criticism takes its own from history. The critic, on the data furnished him by the historian, makes two parts of all his documents. Those that remain after the triple elimination above described go to form the real history; the rest is attributed to the history of the faith or as it is styled, to internal history. For the Modernists distinguish very carefully between these two kinds of history, and it is to be noted that they oppose the history of the faith to real history precisely as real. Thus we have a double Christ: a real Christ, and a Christ, the one of faith, who never really existed; a Christ who has lived at a given time and in a given place, and a Christ who has never lived outside the pious meditations of the believer - the Christ, for instance, whom we find in the Gospel of St. John, which is pure contemplation from beginning to end.

32. But the dominion of philosophy over history does not end here. Given that division, of which We have spoken, of the documents into two parts, the philosopher steps in again with his principle of vital immanence, and shows how everything in the history of the Church is to be explained by vital emanation. And since the cause or condition of every vital emanation whatsoever is to be found in some need, it follows that no fact can ante-date the need which produced it - historically the fact must be posterior to the need. See how the historian works on this principle. He goes over his documents again, whether they be found in the Sacred Books or elsewhere, draws up from them his list of the successive needs of the Church, whether relating to dogma or liturgy or other matters, and then he hands his list over to the critic. The critic takes in hand the documents dealing with the history of faith and distributes them, period by period, so that they correspond exactly with the lists of needs, always guided by the principle that the narration must follow the facts, as the facts follow

the needs. It may at times happen that some parts of the Sacred Scriptures, such as the Epistles, themselves constitute the fact created by the need. Even so, the rule holds that the age of any document can only be determined by the age in which each need had manifested itself in the Church. Further, a distinction must be made between the beginning of a fact and its development, for what is born one day requires time for growth. Hence the critic must once more go over his documents, ranged as they are through the different ages, and divide them again into two parts, and divide them into two lots, separating those that regard the first stage of the facts from those that deal with their development, and these he must again arrange according to their periods.

33. Then the philosopher must come in again to impose on the historian the obligation of following in all his studies the precepts and laws of evolution. It is next for the historian to scrutinise his documents once more, to examine carefully the circumstances and conditions affecting the Church during the different periods, the conserving force she has put forth, the needs both internal and external that have stimulated her to progress, the obstacles she has had to encounter, in a word everything that helps to determine the manner in which the laws of evolution have been fulfilled in her. This done, he finishes his work by drawing up in its broad lines a history of the development of the facts. The critic follows and fits in the rest of the documents with this sketch; he takes up his pen, and soon the history is made complete. Now we ask here: Who is the author of this history? The historian? The critic? Assuredly, neither of these but the philosopher. From beginning to end everything in it is a priori, and a priori in a way that reeks of heresy. These men are certainly to be pitied, and of them the Apostle might well say: They became vain in their thoughts. . . professing themselves to be wise they became fools (Rom. i. 21, 22); but, at the same time, they excite just indignation when they accuse the Church of torturing the texts, arranging and confusing them after its own fashion, and for the needs of its cause. In this they are accusing the Church of something for which their own conscience plainly reproaches them.

How the Bible is Dealt With

34. The result of this dismembering of the Sacred Books and this partition of them throughout the centuries is naturally that the Scriptures can no longer be attributed to the authors whose names they bear. The Modernists have no hesitation in affirming commonly that these books, and especially the Pentateuch and the first three Gospels, have been gradually formed by additions to a primitive brief narration - by interpolations of theological or allegorical interpretation, by transitions, by joining different passages together. This means, briefly, that in the Sacred Books we must admit a vital evolution, springing from and corresponding with evolution of faith. The traces of this evolution, they tell us, are so visible in the books that one might almost write a history of them. Indeed this history they do actually write, and with such an easy security that one might believe them to have with their own eyes seen the writers at work through the ages amplifying the Sacred Books. To aid them in this they call to their assistance that branch of criticism which they call textual, and labour to show that such a fact or such a phrase is not in its right place, and adducing other arguments of the same kind. They seem, in fact, to have constructed for themselves certain types of narration and discourses, upon which they base their decision as to whether a thing is out of place or not. Judge if you can how men with such a system are fitted for practising this kind of criticism. To hear them talk about their works on the Sacred Books, in which they have been able to discover so much that is defective, one would imagine that before them nobody ever even glanced through the pages of Scripture, whereas the truth is that a whole multitude of Doctors, infinitely superior to them in genius, in erudition, in sanctity, have sifted the Sacred Books in every way, and so far from finding imperfections in them, have thanked God more and more the deeper they have gone into them, for His divine bounty in having vouchsafed to speak thus to men. Unfortunately, these great Doctors did not enjoy the same aids to study that are possessed by the Modernists for their guide and rule, - a philosophy borrowed from the negation of God, and a criterion which consists of themselves.

We believe, then, that We have set forth with sufficient clearness the historical method of the Modernists. The philosopher leads the way, the historian follows, and then in due order come internal and textual criticism. And since it is characteristic of the first cause to communicate its virtue to secondary causes, it is quite clear that the criticism We are concerned with is an agnostic, immanentist, and evolutionist criticism. Hence anybody who embraces it and employs it, makes profession thereby of the errors contained in it, and places himself in opposition to Catholic faith. This being so, one cannot but be greatly surprised by the consideration which is attached to it by certain Catholics. Two causes may be assigned for this: first, the close alliance, independent of all differences of nationality or religion, which the historians and critics of this school have formed among themselves; second, the boundless effrontery of these men. Let one of them but open his mouth and the others applaud him in chorus, proclaiming that science has made another step forward; let an outsider but hint at a desire to inspect the new discovery with his own eyes, and they are on him in a body; deny it - and you are an ignoramus; embrace it and defend it - and there is no praise too warm for you. In this way they win over any who, did they but realise what they are doing, would shrink back with horror. The impudence and the domineering of some, and the thoughtlessness and imprudence of others, have combined to generate a pestilence in the air which penetrates everywhere and spreads the contagion. But let us pass to the apologist.

The Modernist as Apologist

35. The Modernist apologist depends in two ways on the philosopher. First, indirectly, inasmuch as his theme is history - history dictated, as we have seen, by the philosopher; and, secondly, directly, inasmuch as he takes both his laws and his principles from the philosopher. Hence that common precept of the Modernist school that the new apologetics must be fed from psychological and historical sources. The Modernist apologists, then, enter the arena by proclaiming to the rationalists that though they are defending religion, they have no intention of employing the data of the sacred books or the histories in current use in the Church, and composed according to old methods, but real history written on modern principles and according to rigorously modern methods. In all this they are not using an argumentum ad hominem, but are stating the simple fact that they hold, that the truth is to be found only in this kind of history. They feel that it is not necessary for them to dwell on their own sincerity in their writings - they are already known to and praised by the rationalists as

49

fighting under the same banner, and they not only plume themselves on these encomiums, which are a kind of salary to them but would only provoke nausea in a real Catholic, but use them as an offset to the reprimands of the Church.

But let us see how the Modernist conducts his apologetics. The aim he sets before himself is to make the non-believer attain that experience of the Catholic religion which, according to the system, is the basis of faith. There are two ways open to him, the objective and the subjective. The first of them proceeds from agnosticism. It tends to show that religion, and especially the Catholic religion, is endowed with such vitality as to compel every psychologist and historian of good faith to recognise that its history hides some unknown element. To this end it is necessary to prove that this religion, as it exists today, is that which was founded by Jesus Christ; that is to say, that it is the product of the progressive development of the germ which He brought into the world. Hence it is imperative first of all to establish what this germ was, and this the Modernist claims to be able to do by the following formula: Christ announced the coming of the kingdom of God, which was to be realised within a brief lapse of time and of which He was to become the Messiah, the divinely-given agent and ordainer. Then it must be shown how this germ, always immanent and permanent in the bosom of the Church, has gone on slowly developing in the course of history, adapting itself successively to the different mediums through which it has passed, borrowing from them by vital assimilation all the dogmatic, cultural, ecclesiastical forms that served its purpose; whilst, on the other hand , it surmounted all obstacles, vanquished all enemies, and survived all assaults and all combats. Anybody who well and duly considers this mass of obstacles, adversaries, attacks, combats, and the vitality and fecundity which the Church has shown throughout them all, must admit that if the laws of evolution are visible in her life they fail to explain the whole of her history - the unknown rises forth from it and presents itself before us. Thus do they argue, never suspecting that their determination of the primitive germ is an a priori of agnostic and evolutionist philosophy, and that the formula of it has been gratuitously invented for the sake of buttressing their position.

36. But while they endeavour by this line of reasoning to secure access for the Catholic religion into souls, these new apologists are

quite ready to admit that there are many distasteful things in it. Nay, they admit openly, and with ill-concealed satisfaction, that they have found that even its dogma is not exempt from errors and contradictions. They add also that this is not only excusable but - curiously enough - even right and proper. In the Sacred Books there are many passages referring to science or history where manifest errors are to be found. But the subject of these books is not science or history but religion and morals. In them history and science serve only as a species of covering to enable the religious and moral experiences wrapped up in them to penetrate more readily among the masses. The masses understood science and history as they are expressed in these books, and it is clear that had science and history been expressed in a more perfect form this would have proved rather a hindrance than a help. Then, again, the Sacred Books being essentially religious, are consequently necessarily living. Now life has its own truth and its own logic, belonging as they do to a different order, viz., truth of adaptation and of proportion both with the medium in which it exists and with the end towards which it tends. Finally the Modernists, losing all sense of control, go so far as to proclaim as true and legitimate everything that is explained by life.

We, Venerable Brethren, for whom there is but one and only truth, and who hold that the Sacred Books, written under the inspiration of the Holy Ghost, have God for their author (Conc. Vat., De Revel., c. 2) declare that this is equivalent to attributing to God Himself the lie of utility or officious lie, and We say with St. Augustine: In an authority so high, admit but one officious lie, and there will not remain a single passage of those apparently difficult to practise or to believe, which on the same most pernicious rule may not be explained as a lie uttered by the author wilfully and to serve a purpose. (Epist. 28). And thus it will come about, the holy Doctor continues, that everybody will believe and refuse to believe what he likes or dislikes. But the Modernists pursue their way gaily. They grant also that certain arguments adduced in the Sacred Books, like those, for example, which are based on the prophecies, have no rational foundation to rest on. But they will defend even these as artifices of preaching, which are justified by life. Do they stop here? No, indeed, for they are ready to admit, nay, to proclaim that Christ Himself manifestly erred in determining the time when the coming of the Kingdom of God was to take place, and they tell us that we must not be surprised at this since even Christ was subject to the laws of life! After this what is to become of the dogmas of the Church? The dogmas brim over with flagrant contradictions, but what matter that since, apart from the fact that vital logic accepts them, they are not repugnant to symbolical truth. Are we not dealing with the infinite, and has not the infinite an infinite variety of aspects? In short, to maintain and defend these theories they do not hesitate to declare that the noblest homage that can be paid to the Infinite is to make it the object of contradictory propositions! But when they justify even contradiction, what is it that they will refuse to justify?

Subjective Arguments

37. But it is not solely by objective arguments that the non-believer may be disposed to faith. There are also subjective ones at the disposal of the Modernists, and for those they return to their doctrine of immanence. They endeavour, in fact, to persuade their non-believer that down in the very deeps of his nature and his life lie the need and the desire for religion, and this not a religion of any kind, but the specific religion known as Catholicism, which, they say, is absolutely postulated by the perfect development of life. And here We cannot but deplore once more, and grievously, that there are Catholics who, while rejecting immanence as a doctrine, employ it as a method of apologetics, and who do this so imprudently that they seem to admit that there is in human nature a true and rigorous necessity with regard to the supernatural order - and not merely a capacity and a suitability for the supernatural, order - and not merely a capacity and a suitability for the supernatural, such as has at all times been emphasized by Catholic apologists. Truth to tell it is only the moderate Modernists who make this appeal to an exigency for the Catholic religion. As for the others, who might be called intergralists, they would show to the non-believer, hidden away in the very depths of his being, the very germ which Christ Himself bore in His conscience, and which He bequeathed to the world. Such, Venerable Brethren, is a summary description of the apologetic method of the Modernists, in perfect harmony, as you may see, with their doctrines - methods and doctrines brimming over with errors, made not for edification but for

destruction, not for the formation of Catholics but for the plunging of Catholics into heresy; methods and doctrines that would be fatal to any religion.

The Modernist as Reformer

38. It remains for Us now to say a few words about the Modernist as reformer. From all that has preceded, some idea may be gained of the reforming mania which possesses them: in all Catholicism there is absolutely nothing on which it does not fasten. Reform of philosophy, especially in the seminaries: the scholastic philosophy is to be relegated to the history of philosophy among obsolete systems, and the young men are to be taught modern philosophy which alone is true and suited to the times in which we live. Reform of theology; rational theology is to have modern philosophy for its foundation, and positive theology is to be founded on the history of dogma. As for history, it must be for the future written and taught only according to their modern methods and principles. Dogmas and their evolution are to be harmonised with science and history. In the Catechism no dogmas are to be inserted except those that have been duly reformed and are within the capacity of the people. Regarding worship, the number of external devotions is to be reduced, or at least steps must be taken to prevent their further increase, though, indeed, some of the admirers of symbolism are disposed to be more indulgent on this head. Ecclesiastical government requires to be reformed in all its branches, but especially in its disciplinary and dogmatic parts. Its spirit with the public conscience, which is not wholly for democracy; a share in ecclesiastical government should therefore be given to the lower ranks of the clergy, and even to the laity, and authority should be decentralised. The Roman Congregations, and especially the index and the Holy Office, are to be reformed. The ecclesiastical authority must change its line of conduct in the social and political world; while keeping outside political and social organization, it must adapt itself to those which exist in order to penetrate them with its spirit. With regard to morals, they adopt the principle of the Americanists, that the active virtues are more important than the passive, both in the estimation in which they must be held and in the exercise of them. The clergy are asked to return to their ancient lowliness and poverty, and

in their ideas and action to be guided by the principles of Modernism; and there are some who, echoing the teaching of their Protestant masters, would like the suppression of ecclesiastical celibacy. What is there left in the Church which is not to be reformed according to their principles?

Modernism and All the Heresies

39. It may be, Venerable Brethren, that some may think We have dwelt too long on this exposition of the doctrines of the Modernists. But it was necessary, both in order to refute their customary charge that We do not understand their ideas, and to show that their system does not consist in scattered and unconnected theories but in a perfectly organised body, all the parts of which are solidly joined so that it is not possible to admit one without admitting all. For this reason, too, We have had to give this exposition a somewhat didactic form and not to shrink from employing certain uncouth terms in use among the Modernists. And now, can anybody who takes a survey of the whole system be surprised that We should define it as the synthesis of all heresies? Were one to attempt the task of collecting together all the errors that have been broached against the faith and to concentrate the sap and substance of them all into one, he could not better succeed than the Modernists have done. Nay, they have done more than this, for, as we have already intimated, their system means the destruction not of the Catholic religion alone but of all religion. With good reason do the rationalists applaud them, for the most sincere and the frankest among the rationalists warmly welcome the modernists as their most valuable allies.

For let us return for a moment, Venerable Brethren, to that most disastrous doctrine of agnosticism. By it every avenue that leads the intellect to God is barred, but the Modernists would seek to open others available for sentiment and action. Vain efforts! For, after all, what is sentiment but the reaction of the soul on the action of the intelligence or the senses. Take away the intelligence, and man, already inclined to follow the senses, becomes their slave. Vain, too, from another point of view, for all these fantasias on the religious sentiment will never be able to destroy common sense, and common sense tells us that emotion and everything that leads the heart captive proves a hindrance instead of a help to the discovery of truth. We speak, of course, of truth in itself - as for that other purely subjective truth, the fruit of sentiment and action, if it serves its purpose for the jugglery of words, it is of no use to the man who wants to know above all things whether outside himself there is a God into whose hands he is one day to fall. True, the Modernists do call in experience to eke out their system, but what does this experience add to sentiment? Absolutely nothing beyond a certain intensity and a proportionate deepening of the conviction of the reality of the object. But these two will never make sentiment into anything but sentiment, nor deprive it of its characteristic which is to cause deception when the intelligence is not there to guide it; on the contrary, they but confirm and aggravate this characteristic, for the more intense sentiment is the more it is sentimental. In matters of religious sentiment and religious experience, you know, Venerable Brethren, how necessary is prudence and how necessary, too, the science which directs prudence. You know it from your own dealings with sounds, and especially with souls in whom sentiment predominates; you know it also from your reading of ascetical books - books for which the Modernists have but little esteem, but which testify to a science and a solidity very different from theirs, and to a refinement and subtlety of observation of which the Modernists give no evidence. Is it not really folly, or at least sovereign imprudence, to trust oneself without control to Modernist experiences? Let us for a moment put the question: if experiences have so much value in their eyes, why do they not attach equal weight to the experience that thousands upon thousands of Catholics have that the Modernists are on the wrong road? It is, perchance, that all experiences except those felt by the Modernists are false and deceptive? The vast majority of mankind holds and always will hold firmly that sentiment and experience alone, when not enlightened and guided by reason, do not lead to the knowledge of God. What remains, then, but the annihilation of all religion, - atheism? Certainly it is not the doctrine of symbolism - will save us from this. For if all the intellectual elements, as they call them, of religion are pure symbols, will not the very name of God or of divine personality be also a symbol, and if this be admitted will not the personality of God become a matter of doubt and the way opened to Pantheism? And to Pantheism that other doctrine of the divine immanence leads directly. For does it, We ask, leave God distinct from man or not? If yes, in what does it differ from Catholic doctrine, and why reject external revelation? If no, we are at once in Pantheism. Now the doctrine of immanence in the Modernist acceptation holds and professes that every phenomenon of conscience proceeds from man as man. The rigorous conclusion from this is the identity of man with God, which means Pantheism. The same conclusion follows from the distinction Modernists make between science and faith. The object of science they say is the reality of the knowable; the object of faith, on the contrary, is the reality of the unknowable. Now what makes the unknowable unknowable is its disproportion with the intelligible - a disproportion which nothing whatever, even in the doctrine of the Modernist, can suppress. Hence the unknowable remains and will eternally remain unknowable to the believer as well as to the man of science. Therefore if any religion at all is possible it can only be the religion of an unknowable reality. And why this religion might not be that universal soul of the universe, of which a rationalist speaks, is something We do see. Certainly this suffices to show superabundantly by how many roads Modernism leads to the annihilation of all religion. The first step in this direction was taken by Protestantism; the second is made by Modernism; the next will plunge headlong into atheism.

THE CAUSE OF MODERNISM

40. To penetrate still deeper into Modernism and to find a suitable remedy for such a deep sore, it behoves Us, Venerable Brethren, to investigate the causes which have engendered it and which foster its growth. That the proximate and immediate cause consists in a perversion of the mind cannot be open to doubt. The remote causes seem to us to be reduced to two: curiosity and pride. Curiosity by itself, if not prudently regulated, suffices to explain all errors. Such is the opinion of Our Predecessor, Gregory XVI., who wrote: A lamentable spectacle is that presented by the aberrations of human reason when it yields to the spirit of novelty, when against the warning of the Apostle it seeks to know beyond what it is meant to know, and when relying too much on itself it thinks it can find the fruit outside the Church wherein truth is found without the slightest shadow of error (Ep. Encycl. Singulari nos, 7 Kal. Jul. 1834).

But it is pride which exercises an incomparably greater sway over the soul to blind it and plunge it into error, and pride sits in Modernism as in its own house, finding sustenance everywhere in its doctrines and an occasion to flaunt itself in all its aspects. It is pride which fills Modernists with that confidence in themselves and leads them to hold themselves up as the rule for all, pride which puffs them up with that vainglory which allows them to regard themselves as the sole possessors of knowledge, and makes them say, inflated with presumption, We are not as the rest of men, and which, to make them really not as other men, leads them to embrace all kinds of the most absurd novelties; it is pride which rouses in them the spirit of disobedience and causes them to demand a compromise between authority and liberty; it is pride that makes of them the reformers of others, while they forget to reform themselves, and which begets their absolute want of respect for authority, not excepting the supreme authority. No, truly, there is no road which leads so directly and so quickly to Modernism as pride. When a Catholic laymen or a priest forgets that precept of the Christian life which obliges us to renounce ourselves if we would follow Jesus Christ and neglects to tear pride from his heart, ah! but he is a fully ripe subject for the errors of Modernism. Hence, Venerable Brethren, it will be your first duty to thwart such proud men, to employ them only in the lowest and obscurest offices; the higher they try to rise, the lower let them be placed, so that their lowly position may deprive them of the power of causing damage. Sound your young clerics, too, most carefully, by yourselves and by the directors of your seminaries, and when you find the spirit of pride among any of them reject them without compunction from the priesthood. Would to God that this had always been done with the proper vigilance and constancy.

41. If we pass from the moral to the intellectual causes of Modernism, the first which presents itself, and the chief one, is ignorance. Yes, these very Modernists who pose as Doctors of the Church, who puff out their cheeks when they speak of modern philosophy, and show such contempt for scholasticism, have embraced the one with all its false glamour because their ignorance of the other has left them without the means of being able to recognise confusion of thought, and to refute sophistry. Their whole system, with all its

errors, has been born of the alliance between faith and false philosophy.

Methods of Propagandism

42. If only they had displayed less zeal and energy in propagating it! But such is their activity and such their unwearying capacity for work on behalf of their cause, that one cannot but be pained to see them waste such labour in endeavouring to ruin the Church when they might have been of such service to her had their efforts been better employed. Their articles to delude men's minds are of two kinds, the first to remove obstacles from their path, the second to devise and apply actively and patiently every instrument that can serve their purpose. They recognise that the three chief difficulties for them are scholastic philosophy, the authority of the fathers and tradition, and the magisterium of the Church, and on these they wage unrelenting war. For scholastic philosophy and theology they have only ridicule and contempt. Whether it is ignorance or fear, or both, that inspires this conduct in them, certain it is that the passion for novelty is always united in them with hatred of scholasticism, and there is no surer sign that a man is on the way to Modernism than when he begins to show his dislike for this system. Modernists and their admirers should remember the proposition condemned by Pius IX: The method and principles which have served the doctors of scholasticism when treating of theology no longer correspond with the exigencies of our time or the progress of science (Syll. Prop. 13). They exercise all their ingenuity in diminishing the force and falsifying the character of tradition, so as to rob it of all its weight. But for Catholics the second Council of Nicea will always have the force of law, where it condemns those who dare, after the impious fashion of heretics, to deride the ecclesiastical traditions, to invent novelties of some kind . . . or endeavour by malice or craft to overthrow any one of the legitimate traditions of the Catholic Church; and Catholics will hold for law, also, the profession of the fourth Council of Constantinople: We therefore profess to conserve and guard the rules bequeathed to the Holy Catholic and Apostolic Church by the Holy and most illustrious Apostles, by the orthodox Councils, both general and local, and by every one of those divine interpreters the Fathers and Doctors of the

Church. Wherefore the Roman Pontiffs, Pius IV. and Pius IX., ordered the insertion in the profession of faith of the following declaration: I most firmly admit and embrace the apostolic and ecclesiastical traditions and other observances and constitutions of the Church. The Modernists pass the same judgment on the most holy Fathers of the Church as they pass on tradition; decreeing, with amazing effrontery that, while personally most worthy of all veneration, they were entirely ignorant of history and criticism, for which they are only excusable on account of the time in which they lived. Finally, the Modernists try in every way to diminish and weaken the authority of the ecclesiastical magisterium itself by sacrilegiously falsifying its origin, character, and rights, and by freely repeating the calumnies of its adversaries. To all the band of Modernists may be applied those words which Our Predecessor wrote with such pain: To bring contempt and odium on the mystic Spouse of Christ, who is the true light, the children of darkness have been wont to cast in her face before the world a stupid calumny, and perverting the meaning and force of things and words, to depict her as the friend of darkness and ignorance, and the enemy of light, science, and progress (Motu-proprio, Ut mysticum, 14 March, 1891). This being so, Venerable Brethren, no wonder the Modernists vent all their gall and hatred on Catholics who sturdily fight the battles of the Church. But of all the insults they heap on them those of ignorance and obstinacy are the favourites. When an adversary rises up against them with an erudition and force that render him redoubtable, they try to make a conspiracy of silence around him to nullify the effects of his attack, while in flagrant contrast with this policy towards Catholics, they load with constant praise the writers who range themselves on their side, hailing their works, excluding novelty in every page, with choruses of applause; for them the scholarship of a writer is in direct proportion to the recklessness of his attacks on antiquity, and of his efforts to undermine tradition and the ecclesiastical magisterium; when one of their number falls under the condemnations of the Church the rest of them, to the horror of good Catholics, gather round him, heap public praise upon him, venerate him almost as a martyr to truth. The young, excited and confused by all this glamour of praise and abuse, some of them afraid of being branded as ignorant, others ambitious to be considered learned, and both classes goaded internally by curiosity and pride, often surrender and give themselves up to Modernism.

43. And here we have already some of the artifices employed by Modernists to exploit their wares. What efforts they make to win new recruits! They seize upon chairs in the seminaries and universities, and gradually make of them chairs of pestilence. From these sacred chairs they scatter, though not always openly, the seeds of their doctrines; they proclaim their teachings without disguise in congresses; they introduce them and make them the vogue in social institutions. Under their own names and under pseudonyms they publish numbers of books, newspapers, reviews, and sometimes one and the same writer adopts a variety of pseudonyms to trap the incautious reader into believing in a whole multitude of Modernist writers - in short they leave nothing untried, in action, discourses, writings, as though there were a frenzy of propaganda upon them. And the results of all this? We have to lament at the sight of many young men once full of promise and capable of rendering great services to the Church, now gone astray. And there is another sight that saddens Us too: that of so many other Catholics, who, while they certainly do not go so far as the former, have yet grown into the habit, as though they had been breathing a poisoned atmosphere, of thinking and speaking and writing with a liberty that ill becomes Catholics. They are to be found among the laity, and in the ranks of the clergy, and they are not wanting even in the last place where one might expect to meet them, in religious institutes. If they treat of biblical questions, it is upon Modernist principles; if they write history, it is to search out with curiosity and to publish openly, on the pretext of telling the whole truth and with a species of ill-concealed satisfaction, everything that looks to them like a stain in the history of the Church. Under the sway of certain a priori rules they destroy as far as they can the pious traditions of the people, and bring ridicule on certain relics highly venerable from their antiquity. They are possessed by the empty desire of being talked about, and they know they would never succeed in this were they to say only what has been always said. It may be that they have persuaded themselves that in all this they are really serving God and the Church - in reality they only offend both, less perhaps by their works themselves than by the spirit in which they write and by the encouragement they are giving to the extravagances of the Modernists.

REMEDIES

44. Against this host of grave errors, and its secret and open advance, Our Predecessor Leo XIII., of happy memory, worked strenuously especially as regards the Bible, both in his words and his acts. But, as we have seen, the Modernists are not easily deterred by such weapons - with an affectation of submission and respect, they proceeded to twist the words of the Pontiff to their own sense, and his acts they described as directed against others than themselves. And the evil has gone on increasing from day to day. We therefore, Venerable Brethren, have determined to adopt at once the most efficacious measures in Our power, and We beg and conjure you to see to it that in this most grave matter nobody will ever be able to say that you have been in the slightest degree wanting in vigilance, zeal or firmness. And what We ask of you and expect of you, We ask and expect also of all other pastors of souls, of all educators and professors of clerics, and in a very special way of the superiors of religious institutions.

I. - The Study of Scholastic Philosophy

45. In the first place, with regard to studies, We will and ordain that scholastic philosophy be made the basis of the sacred sciences. It goes without saying that if anything is met with among the scholastic doctors which may be regarded as an excess of subtlety, or which is altogether destitute of probability, We have no desire whatever to propose it for the imitation of present generations (Leo XIII. Enc. Aeterni Patris). And let it be clearly understood above all things that the scholastic philosophy We prescribe is that which the Angelic Doctor has bequeathed to us, and We, therefore, declare that all the ordinances of Our Predecessor on this subject continue fully in force, and, as far as may be necessary, We do decree anew, and confirm, and ordain that they be by all strictly observed. In seminaries where they may have been neglected let the Bishops impose them and require their observance, and let this apply also to the Superiors of religious institutions. Further let Professors remember that they cannot set St. Thomas aside, especially in metaphysical questions, without grave detriment.

46. On this philosophical foundation the theological edifice is to be solidly raised. Promote the study of theology, Venerable Brethren, by all means in your power, so that your clerics on leaving the seminaries may admire and love it, and always find their delight in it. For in the vast and varied abundance of studies opening before the mind desirous of truth, everybody knows how the old maxim describes theology as so far in front of all others that every science and art should serve it and be to it as handmaidens (Leo XIII., Lett. ap. In Magna, Dec. 10, 1889). We will add that We deem worthy of praise those who with full respect for tradition, the Holy Fathers, and the ecclesiastical magisterium, undertake, with well-balanced judgment and guided by Catholic principles (which is not always the case), seek to illustrate positive theology by throwing the light of true history upon it. Certainly more attention must be paid to positive theology than in the past, but this must be done without detriment to scholastic theology, and those are to be disapproved as of Modernist tendencies who exalt positive theology in such a way as to seem to despise the scholastic.

47. With regard to profane studies suffice it to recall here what Our Predecessor has admirably said: Apply yourselves energetically to the study of natural sciences: the brilliant discoveries and the bold and useful applications of them made in our times which have won such applause by our contemporaries will be an object of perpetual praise for those that come after us (Leo XIII. Alloc., March 7, 1880). But this do without interfering with sacred studies, as Our Predecessor in these most grave words prescribed: If you carefully search for the cause of those errors you will find that it lies in the fact that in these days when the natural sciences absorb so much study, the more severe and lofty studies have been proportionately neglected - some of them have almost passed into oblivion, some of them are pursued in a half-hearted or superficial way, and, sad to say, now that they are fallen from their old estate, they have been dis figured by perverse doctrines and monstrous errors (loco cit.). We ordain, therefore, that the study of natural science in the seminaries be carried on under this law.

II - Practical Application

48. All these prescriptions and those of Our Predecessor are to be borne in mind whenever there is question of choosing directors and professors for seminaries and Catholic Universities. Anybody who in any way is found to be imbued with Modernism is to be excluded without compunction from these offices, and those who already occupy them are to be withdrawn. The same policy is to be adopted towards those who favour Modernism either by extolling the Modernists or excusing their culpable conduct, by criticising scholasticism, the Holy Father, or by refusing obedience to ecclesiastical authority in any of its depositaries; and towards those who show a love of novelty in history, archaeology, biblical exegesis, and finally towards those who neglect the sacred sciences or appear to prefer to them the profane. In all this question of studies, Venerable Brethren, you cannot be too watchful or too constant, but most of all in the choice of professors, for as a rule the students are modelled after the pattern of their masters. Strong in the consciousness of your duty, act always prudently but vigorously.

49. Equal diligence and severity are to be used in examining and selecting candidates for Holy Orders. Far, far from the clergy be the love of novelty! God hates the proud and the obstinate. For the future the doctorate of theology and canon law must never be conferred on anybody who has not made the regular course of scholastic philosophy; if conferred it shall be held as null and void. The rules laid down in 1896 by the Sacred Congregation of Bishops and Regulars for the clerics, both secular and regular, of Italy concerning the frequenting of the Universities, We now decree to be extended to all nations. Clerics and priests inscribed in a Catholic Institute or University must not in the future follow in civil Universities those courses for which there are chairs in the Catholic Institutes to which they belong. If this has been permitted anywhere in the past, We ordain that it be not allowed for the future. Let the Bishops who form the Governing Board of such Catholic Institutes or Universities watch with all care that these Our commands be constantly observed.

III. - Episcopal Vigilance Over Publications

50. It is also the duty of the bishops to prevent writings infected with Modernism or favourable to it from being read when they have been published, and to hinder their publication when they have not. No

book or paper or periodical of this kind must ever be permitted to seminarists or university students. The injury to them would be equal to that caused by immoral reading - nay, it would be greater for such writings poison Christian life at its very fount. The same decision is to be taken concerning the writings of some Catholics, who, though not badly disposed themselves but ill-instructed in theological studies and imbued with modern philosophy, strive to make this harmonize with the faith, and, as they say, to turn it to the account of the faith. The name and reputation of these authors cause them to be read without suspicion, and they are, therefore, all the more dangerous in preparing the way for Modernism.

51. To give you some more general directions, Venerable Brethren, in a matter of such moment, We bid you do everything in your power to drive out of your dioceses, even by solemn interdict, any pernicious books that may be in circulation there. The Holy See neglects no means to put down writings of this kind, but the number of them has now grown to such an extent that it is impossible to censure them all. Hence it happens that the medicine sometimes arrives too late, for the disease has taken root during the delay. We will, therefore, that the Bishops, putting aside all fear and the prudence of the flesh, despising the outcries of the wicked, gently by all means but constantly, do each his own share of this work, remembering the injunctions of Leo XIII. in the Apostolic Constitution Officiorum: Let the Ordinaries, acting in this also as Delegates of the Apostolic See, exert themselves to prescribe and to put out of reach of the faithful injurious books or other writings printed or circulated in their dioceses. In this passage the Bishops, it is true, receive a right, but they have also a duty imposed on them. Let no Bishop think that he fulfils this duty by denouncing to us one or two books, while a great many others of the same kind are being published and circulated. Nor are you to be deterred by the fact that a book has obtained the Imprimatur elsewhere, both because this may be merely simulated, and because it may have been granted through carelessness or easiness or excessive confidence in the author as may sometimes happen in religious Orders. Besides, just as the same food does not agree equally with everybody, it may happen that a book harmless in one may, on account of the different circumstances, be hurtful in another. Should a Bishop, therefore, after having taken the advice of prudent persons, deem it

right to condemn any of such books in his diocese, We not only give him ample faculty to do so but We impose it upon him as a duty to do so. Of course, it is Our wish that in such action proper regard be used, and sometimes it will suffice to restrict the prohibition to the clergy; but even in such cases it will be obligatory on Catholic booksellers not to put on sale books condemned by the Bishop. And while We are on this subject of booksellers, We wish the Bishops to see to it that they do not, through desire for gain, put on sale unsound books. It is certain that in the catalogues of some of them the books of the Modernists are not unfrequently announced with no small praise. If they refuse obedience let the Bishops have no hesitation in depriving them of the title of Catholic booksellers; so too, and with more reason, if they have the title of Episcopal booksellers, and if they have that of Pontifical, let them be denounced to the Apostolic See. Finally, We remind all of the XXVI. article of the abovementioned Constitution Officiorum: All those who have obtained an apostolic faculty to read and keep forbidden books, are not thereby authorised to read books and periodicals forbidden by the local Ordinaries, unless the apostolic faculty expressly concedes permission to read and keep books condemned by anybody.

IV. - Censorship

52. But it is not enough to hinder the reading and the sale of bad books - it is also necessary to prevent them from being printed. Hence let the Bishops use the utmost severity in granting permission to print. Under the rules of the Constitution Officiorum, many publications require the authorisation of the Ordinary, and in some dioceses it has been made the custom to have a suitable number of official censors for the examination of writings. We have the highest praise for this institution, and We not only exhort, but We order that it be extended to all dioceses. In all episcopal Curias, therefore, let censors be appointed for the revision of works intended for publication, and let the censors be chosen from both ranks of the clergy - secular and regular - men of age, knowledge and prudence who will know how to follow the golden mean in their judgments. It shall be their office to examine everything which requires permission for publication according to Articles XLI. and XLII. of the above-mentioned Constitution. The Censor shall give his verdict in writing. If it be

favourable, the Bishop will give the permission for publication by the word Imprimatur, which must always be preceded by the Nihil obstat and the name of the Censor. In the Curia of Rome official censors shall be appointed just as elsewhere, and the appointment of them shall appertain to the Master of the Sacred Palaces, after they have been proposed to the Cardinal Vicar and accepted by the Sovereign Pontiff. It will also be the office of the Master of the Sacred Palaces to select the censor for each writing. Permission for publication will be granted by him as well as by the Cardinal Vicar or his Vicegerent, and this permission, as above prescribed, must always be preceded by the Nihil obstat and the name of the Censor. Only on very rare and exceptional occasions, and on the prudent decision of the bishop, shall it be possible to omit mention of the Censor. The name of the Censor shall never be made known to the authors until he shall have given a favourable decision, so that he may not have to suffer annoyance either while he is engaged in the examination of a writing or in case he should deny his approval. Censors shall never be chosen from the religious orders until the opinion of the Provincial, or in Rome of the General, has been privately obtained, and the Provincial or the General must give a conscientious account of the character, knowledge and orthodoxy of the candidate. We admonish religious superiors of their solemn duty never to allow anything to be published by any of their subjects without permission from themselves and from the Ordinary. Finally We affirm and declare that the title of Censor has no value and can never be adduced to give credit to the private opinions of the person who holds it.

Priests as Editors

53. Having said this much in general, We now ordain in particular a more careful observance of Article XLII. of the above-mentioned Constitution Officiorum. It is forbidden to secular priests, without the previous consent of the Ordinary, to undertake the direction of papers or periodicals. This permission shall be withdrawn from any priest who makes a wrong use of it after having been admonished. With regard to priests who are correspondents or collaborators of periodicals, as it happens not unfrequently that they write matter infected with Modernism for their papers or periodicals,

let the Bishops see to it that this is not permitted to happen, and, should they fail in this duty, let the Bishops make due provision with authority delegated by the Supreme Pontiff. Let there be, as far as this is possible, a special Censor for newspapers and periodicals written by Catholics. It shall be his office to read in due time each number after it has been published, and if he find anything dangerous in it let him order that it be corrected. The Bishop shall have the same right even when the Censor has seen nothing objectionable in a publication.

V. - Congresses

54. We have already mentioned congresses and public gatherings as among the means used by the Modernists to propagate and defend their opinions. In the future Bishops shall not permit Congresses of priests except on very rare occasions. When they do permit them it shall only be on condition that matters appertaining to the Bishops or the Apostolic See be not treated in them, and that no motions or postulates be allowed that would imply a usurpation of sacred authority, and that no mention be made in them of Modernism, presbyterianism, or laicism. At Congresses of this kind, which can only be held after permission in writing has been obtained in due time and for each case, it shall not be lawful for priests of other dioceses to take part without the written permission of their Ordinary. Further no priest must lose sight of the solemn recommendation of Leo XIII.: Let priests hold as sacred the authority of their pastors, let them take it for certain that the sacerdotal ministry, if not exercised under the guidance of the Bishops, can never be either holy, or very fruitful or respectable (Lett. Encyc. Nobilissima Gallorum, 10 Feb., 1884).

VI - Diocesan Watch Committees

55. But of what avail, Venerable Brethren, will be all Our commands and prescriptions if they be not dutifully and firmly carried out? And, in order that this may be done, it has seemed expedient to Us to extend to all dioceses the regulations laid down with great wisdom many years ago by the Bishops of Umbria for theirs.

"In order," they say, "to extirpate the errors already propagated and to prevent their further diffusion, and to remove those teachers of impiety through whom the pernicious effects of such diffusion are being perpetuated, this sacred Assembly, following the example of St. Charles Borromeo, has decided to establish in each of the dioceses a Council consisting of approved members of both branches of the clergy, which shall be charged the task of noting the existence of errors and the devices by which new ones are introduced and propagated, and to inform the Bishop of the whole so that he may take counsel with them as to the best means for nipping the evil in the bud and preventing it spreading for the ruin of souls or, worse still, gaining strength and growth" (Acts of the Congress of the Bishops of Umbria, Nov. 1849, tit 2, art. 6). We decree, therefore, that in every diocese a council of this kind, which We are pleased to name "the Council of Vigilance," be instituted without delay. The priests called to form part in it shall be chosen somewhat after the manner above prescribed for the Censors, and they shall meet every two months on an appointed day under the presidency of the Bishop. They shall be bound to secrecy as to their deliberations and decisions, and their function shall be as follows: They shall watch most carefully for every trace and sign of Modernism both in publications and in teaching, and, to preserve from it the clergy and the young, they shall take all prudent, prompt and efficacious measures. Let them combat novelties of words remembering the admonitions of Leo XIII. (Instruct. S.C. NN. EE. EE., 27 Jan., 1902): It is impossible to approve in Catholic publications of a style inspired by unsound novelty which seems to deride the piety of the faithful and dwells on the introduction of a new order of Christian life, on new directions of the Church, on new aspirations of the modern soul, on a new vocation of the clergy, on a new Christian civilisation. Language of this kind is not to be tolerated either in books or from chairs of learning. The Councils must not neglect the books treating of the pious traditions of different places or of sacred relics. Let them not permit such questions to be discussed in periodicals destined to stimulate piety, neither with expressions savouring of mockery or contempt, nor by dogmatic pronouncements, especially when, as is often the case, what is stated as a certainty either does not pass the limits of probability or is merely based on prejudiced opinion. Concerning sacred relics, let this be the rule: When Bishops, who alone are judges in such matters, know for certain the a relic is not genuine, let them remove it at once from the veneration of the faithful; if the authentications of a relic happen to have been lost through civil disturbances, or in any other way, let it not be exposed for public veneration until the Bishop has verified it. The argument of prescription or well-founded presumption is to have weight only when devotion to a relic is commendable by reason of its antiquity, according to the sense of the Decree issued in 1896 by the Congregation of Indulgences and Sacred Relics: Ancient relics are to retain the veneration they have always enjoyed except when in individual instances there are clear arguments that they are false or suppositions. In passing judgment on pious traditions be it always borne in mind that in this matter the Church uses the greatest prudence, and that she does not allow traditions of this kind to be narrated in books except with the utmost caution and with the insertion of the declaration imposed by Urban VIII, and even then she does not guarantee the truth of the fact narrated; she simply does but forbid belief in things for which human arguments are not wanting. On this matter the Sacred Congregation of Rites, thirty years ago, decreed as follows: These apparitions and revelations have neither been approved nor condemned by the Holy See, which has simply allowed that they be believed on purely human faith, on the tradition which they relate, corroborated by testimonies and documents worthy of credence (Decree, May 2, 1877). Anybody who follows this rule has no cause for fear. For the devotion based on any apparition, in as far as it regards the fact itself, that is to say in as far as it is relative, always implies the hypothesis of the truth of the fact; while in as far as it is absolute, it must always be based on the truth, seeing that its object is the persons of the saints who are honoured. The same is true of relics. Finally, We entrust to the Councils of Vigilance the duty of overlooking assiduously and diligently social institutions as well as writings on social questions so that they may harbour no trace of Modernism, but obey the prescriptions of the Roman Pontiffs.

VII - Triennial Returns

56. Lest what We have laid down thus far should fall into oblivion, We will and ordain that the Bishops of all dioceses, a year after the publication of these letters and every three years thenceforward, furnish the Holy See with a diligent and sworn report

on all the prescriptions contained in them, and on the doctrines that find currency among the clergy, and especially in the seminaries and other Catholic institutions, and We impose the like obligation on the Generals of Religious Orders with regard to those under them.

57. This, Venerable Brethren, is what we have thought it our duty to write to you for the salvation of all who believe. The adversaries of the Church will doubtless abuse what we have said to refurbish the old calumny by which we are traduced as the enemy of science and of the progress of humanity. In order to oppose a new answer to such accusations, which the history of the Christian religion refutes by never failing arguments, it is Our intention to establish and develop by every means in our power a special Institute in which, through the co-operation of those Catholics who are most eminent for their learning, the progress of science and other realms of knowledge may be promoted under the guidance and teaching of Catholic truth. God grant that we may happily realise our design with the ready assistance of all those who bear a sincere love for the Church of Christ. But of this we will speak on another occasion.

58. Meanwhile, Venerable Brethren, fully confident in your zeal and work, we beseech for you with our whole heart and soul the abundance of heavenly light, so that in the midst of this great perturbation of men's minds from the insidious invasions of error from every side, you may see clearly what you ought to do and may perform the task with all your strength and courage. May Jesus Christ, the author and finisher of our faith, be with you by His power; and may the Immaculate Virgin, the destroyer of all heresies, be with you by her prayers and aid. And We, as a pledge of Our affection and of divine assistance in adversity, grant most affectionately and with all Our heart to you, your clergy and people the Apostolic Benediction.

Given at St. Peter's, Rome, on the 8th day of September, 1907, the fifth year of our Pontificate.

PIUS X

SYLLABUS CONDEMNING THE ERRORS OF THE MODERNISTS

LAMENTABILI SANE

Pius X July 3, 1907

With truly lamentable results, our age, casting aside all restraint in its search for the ultimate causes of things, frequently pursues novelties so ardently that it rejects the legacy of the human race. Thus it falls into very serious errors, which are even more serious when they concern sacred authority, the interpretation of Sacred Scripture, and the principal mysteries of Faith. The fact that many Catholic writers also go beyond the limits determined by the Fathers and the Church herself is extremely regrettable. In the name of higher knowledge and historical research (they say), they are looking for that progress of dogmas which is, in reality, nothing but the corruption of dogmas.

These errors are being daily spread among the faithful. Lest they captivate the faithful's minds and corrupt the purity of their faith, His Holiness, Pius X, by Divine Providence, Pope, has decided that the chief errors should be noted and condemned by the Office of this Holy Roman and Universal Inquisition.

Therefore, after a very diligent investigation and consultation with the Reverend Consultors, the Most Eminent and Reverend Lord Cardinals, the General Inquisitors in matters of faith and morals have judged the following propositions to be condemned and proscribed. In fact, by this general decree, they are condemned and proscribed.

1. The ecclesiastical law which prescribes that books concerning the Divine Scriptures are subject to previous examination does not apply to critical scholars and students of scientific exegesis of the Old and New Testament.

2. The Church's interpretation of the Sacred Books is by no means to be rejected; nevertheless, it is subject to the more accurate judgment and correction of the exegetes.

3. From the ecclesiastical judgments and censures passed against free and more scientific exegesis, one can conclude that the Faith the Church proposes contradicts history and that Catholic teaching cannot really be reconciled with the true origins of the Christian religion.

4. Even by dogmatic definitions the Church's magisterium cannot determine the genuine sense of the Sacred Scriptures.

5. Since the deposit of Faith contains only revealed truths, the Church has no right to pass judgment on the assertions of the human sciences.

6. The "Church learning" and the "Church teaching" collaborate in such a way in defining truths that it only remains for the "Church teaching" to sanction the opinions of the "Church learning."

7. In proscribing errors, the Church cannot demand any internal assent from the faithful by which the judgments she issues are to be embraced.

8. They are free from all blame who treat lightly the condemnations passed by the Sacred Congregation of the Index or by the Roman Congregations.

9. They display excessive simplicity or ignorance who believe that God is really the author of the Sacred Scriptures.

10. The inspiration of the books of the Old Testament consists in this: The Israelite writers handed down religious doctrines under a peculiar aspect which was either little or not at all known to the Gentiles.

11. Divine inspiration does not extend to all of Sacred Scriptures so that it renders its parts, each and every one, free from every error.

12. If he wishes to apply himself usefully to Biblical studies, the exegete must first put aside all preconceived opinions about the supernatural origin of Sacred Scripture and interpret it the same as any other merely human document.

13. The Evangelists themselves, as well as the Christians of the second and third generation, artificially arranged the evangelical parables. In such a way they explained the scanty fruit of the preaching of Christ among the Jews.

14. In many narrations the Evangelists recorded, not so much things that are true, as things which, even though false, they judged to be more profitable for their readers.

15. Until the time the canon was defined and constituted, the Gospels were increased by additions and corrections. Therefore there remained in them only a faint and uncertain trace of the doctrine of Christ.

16. The narrations of John are not properly history, but a mystical contemplation of the Gospel. The discourses contained in his Gospel are theological meditations, lacking historical truth concerning the mystery of salvation.

17. The fourth Gospel exaggerated miracles not only in order that the extraordinary might stand out but also in order that it might become more suitable for showing forth the work and glory of the Word Incarnate.

18. John claims for himself the quality of witness concerning Christ. In reality, however, he is only a distinguished witness of the Christian life, or of the life of Christ in the Church at the close of the first century.

19. Heterodox exegetes have expressed the true sense of the Scriptures more faithfully than Catholic exegetes.

20. Revelation could be nothing else than the consciousness man acquired of his revelation to God.

21. Revelation, constituting the object of the Catholic faith, was not completed with the Apostles.

22. The dogmas the Church holds out as revealed are not truths which have fallen from heaven. They are an interpretation of religious facts which the human mind has acquired by laborious effort.

23. Opposition may, and actually does, exist between the facts narrated in Sacred Scripture and the Church's dogmas which rest on them. Thus the critic may reject as false facts the Church holds as most certain.

24. The exegete who constructs premises from which it follows that dogmas are historically false or doubtful is not to be reproved as long as he does not directly deny the dogmas themselves .

25. The assent of faith ultimately rests on a mass of probabilities.

26. The dogmas of the Faith are to be held only according to their practical sense; that is to say, as preceptive norms of conduct and not as norms of believing.

27. The divinity of Jesus Christ is not proved from the Gospels. It is a dogma which the Christian conscience has derived from the notion of the Messias.

28. While He was exercising His ministry, Jesus did not speak with the object of teaching He was the Messias, nor did His miracles tend to prove it.

29. It is permissible to grant that the Christ of history is far inferior to the Christ Who is the object of faith.

30 In all the evangelical texts the name "Son of God" is equivalent only to that of "Messias." It does not in the least way signify that Christ is the true and natural Son of God.

31. The doctrine concerning Christ taught by Paul, John, and the Councils of Nicea, Ephesus and Chalcedon is not that which Jesus taught but that which the Christian conscience conceived concerning Jesus.

32. It is impossible to reconcile the natural sense of the Gospel texts with the sense taught by our theologians concerning the conscience and the infallible knowledge of Jesus Christ.

33 Everyone who is not led by preconceived opinions can readily see that either Jesus professed an error concerning the immediate Messianic coming or the greater part of His doctrine as contained in the Gospels is destitute of authenticity.

34. The critics can ascribe to Christ a knowledge without limits only on a hypothesis which cannot be historically conceived and which is repugnant to the moral sense. That hypothesis is that Christ as man possessed the knowledge of God and yet was unwilling to communicate the knowledge of a great many things to His disciples and posterity.

35. Christ did not always possess the consciousness of His Messianic dignity.

36. The Resurrection of the Savior is not properly a fact of the historical order. It is a fact of merely the supernatural order (neither demonstrated nor demonstrable) which the Christian conscience gradually derived from other facts.

37. In the beginning, faith in the Resurrection of Christ was not so much in the fact itself of the Resurrection as in the immortal life of Christ with God.

38. The doctrine of the expiatory death of Christ is Pauline and not evangelical.

39. The opinions concerning the origin of the Sacraments which the Fathers of Trent held and which certainly influenced their dogmatic canons are very different from those which now rightly exist among historians who examine Christianity .

40. The Sacraments have their origin in the fact that the Apostles and their successors, swayed and moved by circumstances and events, interpreted some idea and intention of Christ.

41. The Sacraments are intended merely to recall to man's mind the ever-beneficent presence of the Creator.

42. The Christian community imposed the necessity of Baptism, adopted it as a necessary rite, and added to it the obligation of the Christian profession.

43. The practice of administering Baptism to infants was a disciplinary evolution, which became one of the causes why the Sacrament was divided into two, namely, Baptism and Penance.

44. There is nothing to prove that the rite of the Sacrament of Confirmation was employed by the Apostles. The formal distinction of the two Sacraments of Baptism and Confirmation does not pertain to the history of primitive Christianity.

45. Not everything which Paul narrates concerning the institution of the Eucharist (I Cor. 11:23-25) is to be taken historically.

46. In the primitive Church the concept of the Christian sinner reconciled by the authority of the Church did not exist. Only very slowly did the Church accustom herself to this concept. As a matter of fact, even after Penance was recognized as an institution of the Church, it was not called a Sacrament since it would be held as a disgraceful Sacrament.

47. The words of the Lord, "Receive the Holy Spirit; whose sins you shall forgive, they are forgiven them; and whose sins you shall retain, they are retained" (John 20:22-23), in no way refer to the Sacrament of Penance, in spite of what it pleased the Fathers of Trent to say.

48. In his Epistle (Ch. 5:14-15) James did not intend to promulgate a Sacrament of Christ but only commend a pious custom. If in this custom he happens to distinguish a means of grace, it is not in that rigorous manner in which it was taken by the theologians who laid down the notion and number of the Sacraments.

49. When the Christian supper gradually assumed the nature of a liturgical action those who customarily presided over the supper acquired the sacerdotal character.

50. The elders who fulfilled the office of watching over the gatherings of the faithful were instituted by the Apostles as priests or bishops to provide for the necessary ordering of the increasing communities and not properly for the perpetuation of the Apostolic mission and power.

51. It is impossible that Matrimony could have become a Sacrament of the new law until later in the Church since it was necessary that a full theological explication of the doctrine of grace and the Sacraments should first take place before Matrimony should be held as a Sacrament.

52. It was far from the mind of Christ to found a Church as a society which would continue on earth for a long course

of centuries. On the contrary, in the mind of Christ the kingdom of heaven together with the end of the world was about to come immediately.

53. The organic constitution of the Church is not immutable. Like human society, Christian society is subject to a perpetual evolution.

54. Dogmas, Sacraments and hierarchy, both their notion and reality, are only interpretations and evolutions of the Christian intelligence which have increased and perfected by an external series of additions the little germ latent in the Gospel.

55. Simon Peter never even suspected that Christ entrusted the primacy in the Church to him.

56. The Roman Church became the head of all the churches, not through the ordinance of Divine Providence, but merely through political conditions.

57. The Church has shown that she is hostile to the progress of the natural and theological sciences.

58. Truth is no more immutable than man himself, since it evolved with him, in him, and through him.

59. Christ did not teach a determined body of doctrine applicable to all times and all men, but rather inaugurated a religious movement adapted or to be adapted to different times and places.

60. Christian Doctrine was originally Judaic. Through successive evolutions it became first Pauline, then Joannine, finally Hellenic and universal.

61. It may be said without paradox that there is no chapter of Scripture, from the first of Genesis to the last of the Apocalypse, which contains a doctrine absolutely identical with that which the Church teaches on the same matter. For the same reason, therefore, no chapter of Scripture has the same sense for the critic and the theologian.

62. The chief articles of the Apostles' Creed did not have the same sense for the Christians of the first ages as they have for the Christians of our time.

63. The Church shows that she is incapable of effectively maintaining evangelical ethics since she obstinately clings to immutable doctrines which cannot be reconciled with modern progress.

64. Scientific progress demands that the concepts of Christian doctrine concerning God, creation, revelation, the Person of the Incarnate Word, and Redemption be re-adjusted.

65. Modern Catholicism can be reconciled with true science only if it is transformed into a non-dogmatic Christianity; that is to say, into a broad and liberal Protestantism.

The following Thursday, the fourth day of the same month and year, all these matters were accurately reported to our Most Holy Lord, Pope Pius X. His Holiness approved and confirmed the decree of the Most Eminent Fathers and ordered that each and every one of the above-listed propositions be held by all as condemned and proscribed.

PETER PALOMBELLI, Notary of the Holy Roman and Universal Inquisition

Table of Contents

THE SYLLABUS OF ERRORS CONDEMNED BY PIUS IX...................................5
    I. PANTHEISM, NATURALISM AND ABSOLUTE RATIONALISM.........5
    II. MODERATE RATIONALISM..6
    III. INDIFFERENTISM, LATITUDINARIANISM..7
    IV. SOCIALISM, COMMUNISM, SECRET SOCIETIES, BIBLICAL
    SOCIETIES, CLERICO-LIBERAL SOCIETIES..7
    V. ERRORS CONCERNING THE CHURCH AND HER RIGHTS..............7
    VI. ERRORS ABOUT CIVIL SOCIETY, CONSIDERED BOTH IN ITSELF
    AND IN ITS RELATION TO THE CHURCH..10
    VII. ERRORS CONCERNING NATURAL AND CHRISTIAN ETHICS....13
    VIII. ERRORS CONCERNING CHRISTIAN MARRIAGE.......................14
    IX. ERRORS REGARDING THE CIVIL POWER OF THE SOVEREIGN
    PONTIFF..15
    X. ERRORS HAVING REFERENCE TO MODERN LIBERALISM...........15
PASCENDI DOMINICI GREGIS...19
    Gravity of the Situation 19
    Division of the Encyclical 21
    ANALYSIS OF MODERNIST TEACHING 21
    Agnosticism its Philosophical Foundation 21
    Vital Immanence 22
    Deformation of Religious History the Consequence 24
    The Origin of Dogmas..26
    Its Evolution..27
    The Modernist as Believer: 28
    Individual Experience and Religious Certitude...................................28
    Religious Experience and Tradition...30
    Faith and Science..30
    Faith Subject to Science..31
    The Methods of Modernists...32
    The Modernist as Theologian: 33
    His Principles, Immanence and Symbolism...33
    Dogma and the Sacraments...35
    The Holy Scriptures...36
    The Church...37
    The Relations Between Church and State..38
    The Magisterium of the Church..39
    The Evolution of Doctrine...41

The Modernist as Historian and Critic.....................................44
    Criticism and its Principles...................................46
    How the Bible is Dealt With....................................47
The Modernist as Apologist..49
Subjective Arguments..52
The Modernist as Reformer...53
Modernism and All the Heresies.................................54
THE CAUSE OF MODERNISM.....................................56
    Methods of Propagandism......................................58
REMEDIES..61
    I. - The Study of Scholastic Philosophy.................61
    II - Practical Application...62
    III. - Episcopal Vigilance Over Publications...........63
    IV. - Censorship...65
    Priests as Editors..66
    V. - Congresses...67
    VI - Diocesan Watch Committees...........................67
    VII - Triennial Returns..69
SYLLABUS CONDEMNING THE ERRORS OF THE MODERNISTS.................71

Made in the USA
Coppell, TX
18 January 2022

71862597R00046